204 SHORT
MONOLOGUES and SCENES
for KIDS and TEENS

**A complete compilation of
all four volumes
of the "51" series
by Dave Kilgore**

Dedicated to all those who share the passion,
pursue the craft, and embody the art.

Copyright ©2016 Dave Kilgore   All rights reserved.
A Scribernaut Press, LLC Publication.
www.scribernautpress.com

204 SHORT MONOLOGUES and SCENES
for KIDS and TEENS

204 Short Monologues and Scenes for Kids and Teens is for young actors to use in practice, in class, for auditions or just for fun. This book contains all 204 pieces from the previous four volumes of the 51 Short Monologues and Scenes for Kids and Teens Series by Dave Kilgore. These books were created to fill the void for acting teachers looking for positive and entertaining very short monologues and scenes for their young student actors.

Talent agents and casting directors want to see what the actor can do in a short amount of time. Thirty to sixty second pieces, like most of the ones in this book, are ideal for that specific reason. Also, this allows the acting student to spend more time focusing on story and character.

The majority of the pieces here are under one minute, allowing for easy memorization and comprehension, while still telling brief stories with entertaining plot twists and allowing the young actor to delve into character, history, relationships and environment.

In this book are many fun pieces you'll be happy to see your own kids and teens performing, knowing they're not just learning to act, but also to tell stories and interact in positive ways.

Some of the pieces in this book are more serious, and allow the young actor to dig deeper and understand the character's journey.

Many of these can be used for guys or gals by simply changing the names, and many can cross into different age ranges by using different scene and character direction.

Be sure to create an imaginary environment conducive to the scene and a history for each role to allow the actor to enter the scene in character.

Building a larger back story around the few lines given in each monologue or scene will help the actor to truly live in the moment and own the scene.

Dave Kilgore is an actor, pianist, film composer, music playwright, novelist, and lover of all the arts. He has written multiple musical plays for kids, short and feature length screenplays and more. A career spanning decades in music, theater, and film, has given him the opportunity to view these crafts from many angles and write short monologues and scenes as clever and concise stories for young actors.

Included in this book...
• Tips on memorization.
• Tips on character development.
• Tips on character interaction.
• 56 Monologues for kids.
• 46 Scenes for kids.
• 60 Monologues for teens
• 42 Scenes for teens.

Enjoy the journey!
Dave Kilgore

A FEW TIPS BEFORE GETTING STARTED

Memorization. Read the monologue or scene slowly, visualizing each line as though you were watching the movie. Observe the scene like you're standing right there, watching and listening to everyone in the scene. When you see something happen in real life, you can tell someone everything you saw, you can tell the story. Doing the same thing with your script will help you with recalling the story and responding with your lines.

Create a history for your character. Just like you, your character's actions, thoughts and personality all come from their own life experience. Figure out where they came from, what they want in the scene, what they're willing to do to get it, what their obstacles may be, and what they may be willing to do to overcome those obstacles. Basically, decide what drives your character.

Already be in character. If you're already in character, in the character's mood, in their frame of mind before the scene starts, then there's no transitioning, or trying to quickly switch into character on a moment's notice. The scene is just a continuance of your character's day.

Be in your character's environment. Use your own life experience to imagine where you are. Is it a school, an office, a warehouse, the deep dark woods, a shopping mall? What are the sights, the sounds, the smells? Is the ground soft, hard, smooth or bumpy? Is it hot, cold, sunny, or raining? Let yourself feel your character's environment.

Who are you in the scene with? Who are you talking to? Is it a very close friend, an old enemy, someone you just met? Are they older, younger? Do either of you have anything you need from the other, or anything to hide?

Most of all, believe your character. Empathize with them. Feel what they feel.

Have the same goals, the same loves, the same pains. As long as you truly believe your character, the better the chance you'll have of making the audience believe.

And that, my friend, is what it's all about.

And now, jump in and have fun with it.

Contents

MONOLOGUES FOR KIDS

SNOW GLOBE

I had this snow globe that I imagined could tell the future. I would shake it up, and all the little snowflakes inside would slowly fall on the little town that was sitting on the bottom of the globe. I would pretend it was a crystal ball, and I could see what was going to happen the next day, or even the next week. Sometimes what I imagined I saw, really happened. Once I shook it really hard and dropped it. It crashed on the floor and there was snow globe everywhere. I didn't see that coming.

NICE TRY

You thought I wouldn't notice what you did. I bet you even thought you were going to get away with it, didn't you? Well, I'm not that easily fooled. I thought that looked like an awfully big pile of mashed potatoes on my plate. So I looked, and sure enough, you were hiding broccoli under there. Nice try, Mom. Nice try.

RAIN

The rain makes me sad. Especially on the weekend, when I don't have school. It's darker and chillier than a sunny day. I have to stay inside so I don't get wet and catch a cold. But when the rain is finally over, and the sun comes out, I love running outside to look for rainbows. Sometimes, the best things are worth waiting for.

BIG STAR

I'm going to be in movies. I'm going to be a big star, make lots of money, and everyone will want my autograph. There will be red carpets, movie premieres, and newspaper reporters with cameras following me everywhere. Well, I like movies, but I don't want anyone to see me trip on the red carpet, and I really don't know if I want all those cameras pointed at me. Maybe I'll be a writer instead. A newspaper reporter. Yeah, I think I'd like that.

BIRTHDAY PARTY

Tommy's the boy next door. My mom invited him to my birthday party last year, but he didn't want to come, 'cause I'm a girl. That's okay, when I grow up, I'm gonna be a stunt woman in movies, and I won't let Tommy ride my motorcycle. Let's see how he likes that!

SLOW TIME

I've been watching the clock on the wall, and it's going really, really slow. It seemed to go really fast when I was playing ball in the house and broke my mom's favorite vase. But not now. Now it's like someone took the batteries out of the clock or something. Maybe that's why they call it a time out!

NIAGARA FALLS

I went on vacation with my family last year. We went to Niagara Falls. We went on a boat ride, walking through caves that came out under the falls, strolling along the river, and saw all the colored lights on the falls at night. Yeah, the very best part, was the pizza. And the ice cream. That was a great vacation.

MONSTERS UNDER THE BED

Did you know that the monster under your bed isn't really there? There's really nothing to worry about. We're often afraid of what we can't see, and until someone shows us that the monsters aren't really there, we get scared and hide under the covers. Last year, when I was a kid, I would do that. But now that I'm a lot older, I know I don't have to be afraid. Trust me, there are no monsters under your bed. They're in the closet!
Roooaaarrrrrrr!!!!

MY DOG SPARKY

My dog, Sparky, is my best friend. He always sits with me when I get ready for school in the morning, and he's always there to meet me when I get home. If the bully next door picks on me, Sparky runs up and barks at him until he runs away. And best of all, he doesn't get mad at me for not doing my homework and telling my teacher that my dog ate it. Sparky's the coolest dog ever.

TREES

Did you ever climb a really tall tree? I mean, really, really tall? It can be fun, but it can be scary when you get up high and can't get back down. When I'm older, I'm going to get a job where I have to learn how to climb trees safely, and I get to do it every day, and they pay me to do it. For now, I think I'll just enjoy lying on the grass and looking up at them. Trees are so cool!

SCARY BASEMENT

My basement is really scary. It's big, it's dark, and it makes weird noises. If I have to go down there by myself, it really creeps me out. My dad says there's nothing to worry about, that I'm just being silly. So I decided to make a game out of it. It's big and dark because it's an ancient cave, full of buried treasure. The weird noises are the ghosts of friendly pirates, telling me where the treasure is. Yeah, maybe I'm a little silly, but sometimes, silly is fun!

SCARIEST THING

It was the scariest thing I'd ever seen. My heart almost stopped when I saw it! It was hairy, it was green, and it screamed really loud like a wild animal. I surprised it, and it chased me all through my house and out the front door. I fell down on the grass in my front yard, laughing like crazy! It was my sister, wearing green beauty cream on her face! She looked so funny!

MATH TEST

Hey, did you hear what happened to Sally? She got an "F" on her math test today! That's so funny! She thinks she's so smart, always getting the best grades, top of the class, always handing in her homework early. Ha! Not any more! This time I got the "A+", and she didn't. Oh, wait, what's this? This is Sally's math test! She's got mine! I got the "F"! Arrrrggggghhhhh!

LUNCHBOX

I don't know why Tommy thinks he's so cool. He brings a bag lunch. Can you believe that? A stupid little brown bag, crinkled, folded over at the top, easy to poke holes in, and his peanut butter and jelly sandwich probably gets smashed and gooey all the time. Now, my Teenage Mutant Ninja Turtles lunchbox, that's cool. And it would be even cooler, if I hadn't lost it.

KITTY CAT

I don't know why my kitty cat keeps meowing at me. I don't know what he wants, and I didn't do anything. I'm just sitting here, minding my own business, eating a tuna fish sandwich. Ooooohhhh, tuna! No, mittens, this is my tuna! Oh, okay, just a little. Meow to you, too!

HOMEWORK

Where's my homework? Well, you see, I was planning on doing my homework, but when I got home last night, an airplane had landed on my front lawn, and it blocked my front door, so I couldn't get in. Then, when I tried to get in the back door, an army of ninja fighters were having this huge birthday party in my back yard, and I couldn't get past them. By the time the aliens beamed the airplane up to their spaceship, and I was finally able to get in the front door, it was late, and my mom sent me to bed without any dinner. So, can I go to lunch now?

HOMEWORK MACHINE

Did you ever have to do something you really didn't want to do? I mean, like, eating your vegetables, or raking leaves, or doing your homework? One day, when I'm old enough, I'm going to invent a machine that does all that stuff for me. But not right now. I don't have time. I have to eat my vegetables, rake the leaves, and do my homework.

GHOST STORIES

I have a friend who is a ghost. I mean, he's not really a ghost, I like to think he's a ghost. I pretend he hangs around and tells me stories about when he was alive. Like maybe he was a pirate, sailing the seven seas, or a brave prince, fighting dragons and rescuing damsels in distress. Really, he's my imagination, and he helps me to come up with all these really cool stories. I like that I can do that. When I write a story for you, I hope you'll like it, too.

FAVORITE SPORT

What's my favorite sport? Baseball! I get to swing a big stick and run around the bases. Except when I swing the big stick three times and the umpire yells, "Strike three, you're out!" Then my favorite sport is hockey. I get to swing a big stick and skate around the ice. Except when I fall down. Hey! Maybe my favorite sport is swinging a big stick!

BORROWED THINGS

I get so mad when my sister borrows my things. She never puts them back where she found them, and I can never find them when I need them. So I got myself a big box with a latch, put all my stuff inside the box, and put a combination lock on it, so she can't get into it. But now I can't remember the combination! Oh, well. At least I know where all my stuff is now.

FRISBEE

My friends and I went to the park the other day to play Frisbee. I threw the Frisbee really hard, and this dog caught it and started running with it! My friends started chasing the dog to get our Frisbee back, but the dog came running straight at me! I thought he was going to attack me! Then the dog stopped right in front of me and dropped the Frisbee at my feet and wagged his tail. He thought we were playing fetch! Me, my friends and that dog played together the rest of the day.

CHORES

It hurts me. It really hurts me when you say that I don't care, or that I am not responsible. You know I want to do nice things for you. You know I want to help around the house and take the garbage out, but there are much more important things that I have to do. So I'll do that when I get back from playing baseball with my friends. (pause) Um…okay, mom. I'll do it now. Baseball will just have to wait.

PICNIC

I was really hoping more kids my age would come to the picnic. My parents and all their family and friends showed up, ate hot dogs and hamburgers, played a few games, but mostly just sat around talking all day. The older kids went off by themselves. The younger kids couldn't keep up with me. Maybe next year will be different. Maybe then I'll be old enough to hang out with the older kids. After the hot dogs and hamburgers, of course.

DINOSAURS

Did you know that dinosaurs were here and gone way long before we were? People never got to see real dinosaurs in the old times. Until movies came along, people didn't get to see them, get chased by them, or get eaten by them. But now, we get to do all that stuff, in movies. I just wonder where the movie makers found all those dinosaurs. They must have some special pet store where they buy them. I wanna go there someday. As long as they don't eat me.

OLYMPIC CHAMPION

I'm trying out for the school track team. I'm gonna be the fastest runner, the highest jumper, and the farthest thrower. I plan on breaking every school record, and one day being in the Olympics. I'll be the world's greatest Olympic champion ever. And I know I can, because I have faith in me. I'll work hard, I'll be a leader, and I'll show everyone that they can be champions, too. Because it's great to be a winner, and it's great to help other people be winners. Or, maybe I'll be a teacher. Because they do that, too.

BASEBALL GLOVE

I just want you to say you're sorry. And I want you to mean it. Don't just say it. That was my favorite baseball glove, and you lost it, Dad. I had it broken in just the way I like it, and now I'm gonna have to get a new one and break it in all over again. Um, I can get a new one, right? No? Um, that's okay. I just remembered where I put my old one. Never mind.

GIRLFRIEND

When I said I liked her, I didn't mean that I LIKED HER, liked her. I meant that I liked her as a friend. That she was pretty cool, for a girl. Now the other kids think she's my girlfriend. When she hears about that, I hope she doesn't get mad at me. I mean, after all, she is my friend. And she's pretty cool. For a girl. Maybe next year she'll be my girlfriend. That would be cool.

BACK PACK

I didn't want to go home. I knew I was going to be in so much trouble when I got there. I lost my back pack, and I had no idea what I could have done with it. I was at school all day, and didn't even remember bringing it to class. I was sure my parents would be so mad at me. So when I got home, before I walked in the door, I was ready to start apologizing and pleading for my life. Then, when I went in, there it was, sitting on the couch! I forgot to take it to school with me that morning! Whew!

FRED DANGER

Fred Danger here. Defender of the universe and friend to all. If you're ever in trouble, want a helping hand, or just need a friend to talk to, I'm your man. Everyone has a time in their life when they need help and don't know what to do or who to call. Anything you need, I will step up, and lend an ear, stand for justice, or mow your lawn. I will be your hero. Righteousness is my reward. And my rates are pretty reasonable, too.

TREASURE HUNT

My friend and I went treasure hunting. He borrowed his dad's metal detector, and we went to the park to see what we could dig up. I imagined finding gold rings, old coins, and maybe some long lost pirate treasure. We were both pretty excited about it. We worked all day long, taking turns swinging that metal detector back and forth. Beep. Beep. Beep. We hunted and dug and filled our sacks. Total for the day? One quarter, two dimes, three nickels, and seventy three bottle caps. Seventy cents! That's thirty-five cents each! Not bad for a day's work, I'd say.

OUTRAGEOUS CAKE

That was the largest, most ridiculous, outrageous birthday cake I've
ever seen. Jason's birthday was last week, and his mom made him
invite me to the party. I'm sure he didn't want to, seeing as how
we've never really been friends. But his mom and my mom are
friends, so I got invited. Anyway, I always knew that Jason was
spoiled and got whatever he wanted. He told his mom he wanted the
biggest birthday cake the bakery could make, and she got it for him.
Then when it was time to cut the cake, he didn't want to share it with
anyone at the party. Well, Jason got everything he asked for, and
more. All the gifts, all the balloons, and all the cake. He somehow
ate the whole thing. He also got to stay home from school the next
day, because he was so sick. I guess that's what happens when you
don't share.

COMPUTER VIRUS

I decided to help my parents with a problem I found out they've had
lately. They were both angry and grumpy and couldn't get their work
done because they said their computer caught a virus. That sounds
pretty serious to me. But as important as it seems that the computer
gets better, I'm really more concerned about my mom and dad. Since
they work on the computer so much, and the computer has a virus, I
was afraid they might catch the virus, too. So, I got a box a tissues
and some sanitary wipes from the closet and put them next to the
computer. My parents said that was very thoughtful, and will protect
them. Yeah, I'm pretty proud of myself.

LOST IN THE WOODS

You want to know what the scariest time of my life was? It was last year, when I was a kid. I was taking a walk through the woods that are just down the block from my house. I was daydreaming, thinking about how I wanted to be a secret agent or something when I grow up, and wasn't paying attention to where I was walking. I looked around, and nothing was familiar. The trees were different, there was a creek up ahead, and I heard weird noises from the woods. I almost freaked out, thinking I was lost, and then I figured it out. All I had to do was turn around and go back the way I came. There was only one path. But yeah, it was scary for a moment.

NEW ZOMBIE

I was talking with my friend Andy the other day about how to know who's a zombie and who isn't. He said you have to look at how they walk, and how they talk, and if they have skin falling off of them or not. I agreed that those could be easy ways to recognize a zombie, but I also said that you really have to look closer than that. I mean, if they're new zombies, maybe they aren't falling apart that much or acting that weird yet. Sometimes, you just gotta really pay attention. Mrs. Barkley, the old lady that works in the cafeteria at school, might be a zombie. I would have kept watching her to be sure, but I had to quit when she got weirded out and told me to stop staring at her.

NOT SLEEPY

Don't worry, I'm not sleepy. I got plenty of sleep last night. I didn't really mean to, though. I was out all day yesterday playing with my new puppy, and I think we wore each other out. I didn't feel tired or anything when we went inside, but my mom told me I needed to go to bed. I begged her to let me stay up because I was having so much fun with Scruffy. Scruffy, he's our puppy. He can run and bounce and play like you wouldn't believe. Anyway, I told my mom that I wasn't sleepy, and she said I could stay up for another hour. So, I laid down on the floor with Scruffy, and the next thing I remember, I was in my bed and it was morning. I guess maybe I was a little sleepy. But I'm not now.

ZOO COOKIES

My whole class went to the zoo last week. Mrs. Emory, she's my science teacher, she said that we were not allowed to feed the animals. Well, I almost got in trouble because one of the other kids tattled on me. I mean, I wasn't feeding the lions, or the tigers, or the bears, or the penguins, or anything big and scary in the cages. I was eating a chocolate chip cookie, and a big piece fell off and landed on the ground. Before I could pick it up, a bird flew down and got it. It was an accident, but Charlie thought he'd tell the teacher anyway. I didn't get in trouble, but from now on, I'm watching what I do around Charlie. You can't get away with anything around that guy.

AUTUMN

I always feel sad in the fall. A little, anyway. Autumn reminds me of where I used to live, where in the fall we always got to drink apple cider and take hay rides on the farm that had the old cider mill. I had some good friends there, and we'd always go to the farm together. We'd pile in one of the dad's minivans and sing songs all the way there and back. I have some new friends where we live now, but I'm always going to miss the old ones. But if we have to move again, I'm sure I'll miss the friends I've made here, and I'll make new ones again wherever we go. I do have some great memories, though. This autumn, I'm sure I'll make more.

GOOD DEED GONE WRONG

Sometimes, the best intentions take you in the wrong direction. My friend, Allen, needed my help. He said that he liked this girl named Becky, and he was too shy to tell her. He wanted me to talk to her and let her know that he liked her, a lot. So I did. But Becky got upset with me, and ran away crying. I didn't understand, because I thought I was doing a good thing. Then one of Becky's friends told me that Becky had just asked her to tell me that Becky liked me, a lot. Oh, boy. What a mess!

WHY WAR?

I don't understand why adults do some of the things they do. Particularly, war. When I get in trouble for doing something I shouldn't, I get punished, and my parents tell me I shouldn't have done what I did, because I knew it was wrong. Adults know that war is wrong. Why do they still do it? Who's there to punish them and tell them they shouldn't have done it? I hope, when I get older, more people will think the way I do, and we can stop making wars. I think that would make the world a much nicer place.

SHADOW OF DOUBT

Did you ever know that something was true, even if you didn't have any proof? You look around, check out the evidence, and come to the conclusion that there's that one person you just know for sure, beyond the shadow of a doubt, who is responsible for a crime? Yeah, well, that happened at my house. My mom made a whole batch of chocolate chip cookies, and someone was accused of eating every last one. Me! They accused me! Can you believe that? There were no witnesses, and no evidence. Well, except for the chocolate on my fingers and the cookie crumbs on my shirt. You call that proof? Hmm. Maybe I need to talk to my attorney.

KID OF THE MONTH

I think there should be a Kid of the Month award, for kids who go above and beyond the call of duty. Something special for some really great kid who picks up all the dishes after dinner, helps fold the laundry, helps out with the gardening, and shovels the snow in the winter. Oh, and gets all his homework done on time. Yeah, I think that would be a really nice award to have. And maybe someday, I'll do all those things, and I'll get that award. Yeah, someday.

NO CRYING

I know you're not supposed to cry over little things. You should take the bad with the good, hold your head up, be strong, all that kind of stuff that they say. But sometimes, it's not easy. My best friend in the whole world just moved away to a whole other state. We'll probably never see each other again. I don't think that's a little thing. Not to me. I'm really going to miss my best bud. So yes, sometimes, I cry. I can't help it. And I think my friend does, too. Maybe that just shows how much you care about someone. But someday, we'll meet again, and I'll probably cry because I'm happy. That'll be okay.

BACK IN TIME

I've been all over the internet, looking for instructions on how to build a time machine. It's really important that I build one, and I need to do it fast. You see, this afternoon, I was taking my bike out of the garage, and I guess I didn't have enough room. I was in a hurry and wasn't watching, and my bike pedal put a big, long, ugly scratch all the way down my dad's car. Not the one he drives to work. The nineteen sixty-five Mustang he just finished restoring. So you see, I need a time machine, so I can go back in time and tell him not to buy that car. Or, maybe wait to take my bike out, I guess.

SIBLING JUSTICE

My little brother is going to be in so much trouble. Last week, I got blamed for spilling milk on my parent's sofa, and it wasn't me who did it. It was my little brother, but he said it was me, and my parents believed him. So today, I ran around the back yard in my tennis shoes and tracked mud all over my mom's new white living room carpet. When she gets home, I'll tell her that he did it. She'll be so mad. Wait, my shoes are much bigger than my little brother's shoes. Maybe my mom won't notice the size of the mud prints. Oh, boy. I'm going to be in so much trouble.

THE PRETENDER

Sometimes I like to pretend I'm other people. Some kids like to pretend they're astronauts, or firemen, or movie stars, or secret agents, or even the President of the United States. Sometimes they play cops and robbers. All kinds of things like that. I sometimes pretend I'm one of those handicapped kids I see. Not to make fun of them. I want to feel what it's like to go through the struggles they go through. I can't imagine it's easy for them, and I want to understand life from their point of view. I hope that if I can do that, that I will do a better job of making them feel comfortable and helping them whenever I can.

ALL-STAR POET

I'm a top all-star poet, and you may not know it, but I'm also a pretty good actor. So when casting the part, know I act from the heart, and that is a really big factor. Also, you see, if you decide on me, I'll learn my lines really fast. And then best of all, I'll be on the ball, and bring doughnuts for the entire cast. That is, if my mom will let me. And if she'll pay for them. I really want this role!

BODY CHECK

A few years ago, I was ice skating at the local rink. It was my first time out, so of course I was going really slow, trying not to fall down. I spent most of my time hanging on to the wall, figuring out how to stay up and move forward. When I finally felt confident enough, I skated away from the wall, and I was doing pretty well, until the rink bully skated by. He clipped me really hard from behind, and I landed on the ice on my knees. It hurt so bad I couldn't stand up for like, five minutes. But since then, he's been banned from the rink, and I've become a pretty good skater myself. But I'll never do what he did. I'm a much better person than that.

FAIRY TALES

My mom used to read me fairy tales when I was younger, and that was a lot of fun. There were dragons, and princes and princesses, and flying horses, and castles. Those were really cool. Sometimes there were monsters. Those stories scared me a little bit, but not too much. I know now that most of those stories aren't true, but I still think of them sometimes and smile. One day, when I'm older, I'll read those same stories to my kids. It'll be fun to share those stories and watch them smile, too.

HE-MAN

Yeah, I work out. You know, lifting weights and stuff. Barbells, dumbbells, dinner bells, all kinds of bells. I could probably lift a car, but I don't want to show off. I mean, not a bus or a truck or a tank. Nothing that big. A regular car. Not a big one. One of those smaller ones. A compact car. Not a four door. A two door maybe. Or one with no doors. Like, a bicycle. Yeah, I can lift my bicycle. But I don't want to show off.

ART CLASS

I'm one of the best students in my art class, in case you didn't know. I draw and paint. Mostly watercolor. I have my own style. Very unique, I'm told. Last week, I painted a really nice, realistic painting of a horse. I thought it looked so real, that I could just step right into that painting and ride that horse away. I asked the teacher what he thought my style was, and he said it was abstract. I don't know what that means, but I'm sure the teacher was blown away by it, because he was shaking his head when he walked away. Yeah, I'm a pretty darned good artist.

BROKE GIRLS

My girlfriend and I went to the movies last week. When we got there, we realized that we didn't have enough money for two tickets. So we bought one ticket, and took turns going in and out of the theater every ten minutes. That way, when we got home, we could tell each other what we saw and it was like we both saw the whole movie. Problem was, she lost the ticket before we could see the end of the movie. Now we'll never know if the Titanic sank or not.

STUFFED TOY

Yeah, I know, I'm way too old to play with stuffed animal toys. And I don't. Not really. It's just that, there was this one, this white teddy bear I had when I was a little kid, that was my favorite. My mom bought it for me when I was at the hospital getting my tonsils out. And after that, whenever I skinned my knee, or just didn't feel well, she would always bring it to me. It always made me feel better. So, you see, I don't play with it now, but I do keep it around, because it reminds me that no matter what happens, I can still find a reason to smile.

DETECTIVE MORGAN

Last month, my bike went missing, and I called the police. I was pretty frantic on the phone, so they sent out this lady detective to investigate. Detective Morgan was very thorough. She asked me all kinds of questions like, do I have any enemies, and do I have any idea who may have taken it, and have I seen anyone else in the neighborhood riding my bike. I said "No" to all those questions. She then asked me where I had seen it last. That's when I remembered, I had it in the back yard, greasing up the chain the day before. The detective took me out back, and there it was, right where I had left it. That was really embarrassing. Next time my bike is missing, I think I'll check there first.

CATS AND DOGS

I think there should be a rule, that all cats and dogs live as long as people do. It's not fair when you have a pet that is like a family member, like a best friend, and they have to go away before you do. It's very sad. It makes your heart hurt. My cat, Casey, was my very best friend. I loved him so much, but he had to go away. I have two more cats now, and I love them, too. And I know it'll hurt when they have to leave. So, I guess the best thing I can do is to treat them as nice as I can, and let them know how much they are loved. Then they will have had happy lives, and I guess that'll make it okay. I still miss my Casey. He was the best.

TRACK STAR

I'm the fastest guy on the track team. I run the hundred yard dash, the two-twenty, and the high hurdles. I practice every day after school, so I can be the best. You have to practice if you want to be good at anything. But the best practice I get is at home. All I have to do is make fun of my big sister, and she chases me all over the house. I run, I jump over furniture, and it usually takes a while before she catches me. That's when I realize, I'm a track star, but not a very good wrestler. She pins me every time.

BIRTHDAY SURPRISE

Last week was my birthday. My parents had a party for me and invited a lot of my friends. We had the usual, hot dogs, cake, and ice cream. Then everyone gathered around while I opened my gifts. I got a lot of cool stuff, I guess, but nothing I really wanted. Not what I had asked for. Then my dad went out to the garage and came back in with a box with holes in it and a bow on top, and set it in front of me. The box moved all on its own, and I heard a puppy barking from inside it. Best...birthday...ever!

SCENES FOR KIDS

BEST PIZZA EVER

MAGGIE and LISA are sitting on the front porch.

MAGGIE
Hey, Lisa, you wanna go to the mall with me and my parents? We're gonna get pizza in the food court for lunch.

LISA
No. My mom's making homemade pizza for dinner tonight.

MAGGIE
Cool! Pizza for lunch *and* dinner?

LISA
No. Not cool. My mom's pizza is way better than the pizza at the mall. Hers is the best pizza ever.

MAGGIE
What's wrong with that?

LISA
If I fill up on mall pizza, then I don't eat that much of my mom's pizza, she'll think I don't like hers anymore, and she'll stop making it.

MAGGIE
Then maybe I can share some of my mall pizza with you, we'll both have just a little, so we don't get stuffed, and then we can come back to your house at dinner time and eat your mom's pizza.

LISA
No, that won't work either.

MAGGIE
Why not?

LISA
Like I said, my mom's pizza is the best, and I'm not sharing!

END

DETENTION

ETHAN and MARKUS are sitting in detention.

ETHAN
I can't believe I'm stuck in detention again.

MARKUS
What don't you believe, Ethan? You knocked the teacher's books all over the floor.

ETHAN
But it wasn't my fault.

MARKUS
How could it not be your fault? You pushed the books off with both hands. Everybody saw it.

ETHAN
I tripped. I was trying to catch myself.

MARKUS
How did you trip?

ETHAN
While I was walking to the front of the room, I turned to make a monster face at Chrissy, and someone must have put their foot out and tripped me. I didn't see who it was.

MARKUS
Imagine that.

ETHAN
What are you here for, Markus?

MARKUS
The teacher saw me stick my foot out and trip you.

END

LOST HOMEWORK

STEVEN and PAUL are sitting in back of the class.

STEVEN
Hey, Paul. Did you see my homework?

PAUL
No, did you lose it?

STEVEN
No, I just don't know where it is.

PAUL
Well, Steven, if you don't know where it is, doesn't that mean you lost it?

STEVEN
No. It means I don't know where it is right now.

PAUL
Soooo, you lost your homework.

STEVEN
Will you say that to the teacher?

PAUL
Why don't you tell her yourself?

STEVEN
Because I would be lying. You could just repeat to the teacher what you heard me say.

PAUL
Wait, why would you be lying?

STEVEN
Because I didn't do my homework!

PAUL
Teacher! Steven didn't do his homework!

STEVEN
Thanks a lot.

END

STAGE FRIGHT
JENNY and KYLE are standing backstage before the play.

JENNY
Kyle, do you know all your lines?

KYLE
Of course I do, Jenny. I'm a professional.

JENNY
That's really cool. I get a little stage fright before I get on stage.

KYLE
Not me. I've been doing this all my life. I'm what they call a natural.

JENNY
Natural what?

KYLE
Actor, silly! I was born for the stage. I know that when I get out there, it's
all about the performance. It's about making the audience believe that my
character is real. And when I step out on the stage, I step into character.
From there on, it's clear sailing.

JENNY
Wow. It must be nice to be so professional. I'll bet you're going to make it
big!

KYLE
You know it, kiddo! Hey, there's our cue. Let's go.

JENNY
Good luck!

Jenny kisses Kyle on the cheek and steps forward. Kyle steps forward, and
stops, wide eyed, frozen in fear.

JENNY (CONT'D)
Kyle, are you okay? Kyle? Kyle?
(smiles toward the audience)
Thank you! And now, intermission.

END

WHEN I GROW UP

BEV and LAURIE are sitting in back of the class.

BEV
Hey, Laurie. What's wrong? You look depressed.

LAURIE
I don't know what I want to be when I grow up, and my brother is always bugging me about it.

BEV
So. Big deal. Most of us don't know what we want to be.

LAURIE
But my brother says he wants to be an astronaut when he grows up, and he's only a year older than me.

BEV
Okay. So?

LAURIE
So, if I don't decide what I want to be soon, I can't prepare now, and when we grow up, he'll be an astronaut, and I won't be anything.

BEV
Hey, maybe you could be an astronaut, too. That way, when you grow up, you and your brother can go into space together.

LAURIE
Bev, you're the best friend ever. You always know the right thing to say.

BEV
Yup, I do, don't I?

LAURIE
Yup, when I grow up, I'll be a fireman, for sure.

BEV
Oh, brother.

END

STUTTERING

CARLEY and DENISE are talking on the playground.

CARLEY
Denise, did you hear Gina talking?

DENISE
Yeah.

CARLEY
Sh-sh-she stutters.

DENISE
Yeah, so.

CARLEY
So, don't you think she sounds funny?

DENISE
No, Carley. I think she sounds like she has a problem talking. That's
nothing to make fun of.

CARLEY
So why are you so sensitive about it?

DENISE
What if you stuttered? How would you like it if I made fun of you?

CARLEY
But I don't stutter.

DENISE
You're a bad speller. Would you like it if I made fun of you for that?

CARLEY
No.

DENISE
Okay, then. Let's invite Gina to our sleepover tonight. And no poking fun.

CARLEY
You go it.

END

BAG LUNCH

FRANK and CARLA are sitting in the lunchroom at school. Carla is staring at Frank.

FRANK
Isn't there anything you'd rather be doing than bugging me?

CARLA
Nope.

FRANK
Don't you have somewhere else to be?

CARLA
Nope.

FRANK
Don't you have any other friends?

CARLA
Just you, Frank. As far as I'm concerned, you're the only other person in the whole world right now.

FRANK
Really? Why me? Do you like me or something? I mean, it would be okay if you do. I, I, kind of think you're, you know, cute.

CARLA
No. You grabbed my lunch by mistake. I'd like it back now.

FRANK
Oh, silly me! I'm so sorry. Here, Carla.

CARLA
And don't do it again.

Carla grabs her lunch bag and walks away.

FRANK
Yup, it worked! I got Carla to talk to me! Yeah!

END

SLOWING DOWN

MARGIE and BRENDA are sitting under a tree, talking.

MARGIE
Brenda, I think I'm getting old.

BRENDA
Why do you say that?

MARGIE
I just can't run as fast as I used to.

BRENDA
But, you're a fast runner, Margie. You were always one of the fastest on the track team.

MARGIE
Yeah, but lately, I seem to be slowing down.

BRENDA
How do you know that? Have you timed yourself?

MARGIE
Nope. It's just that, well, you know that boy Zeke, the one that keeps chasing me and pulling my hair?

BRENDA
Yeah, the cute one.

MARGIE
Yeah, him. Well, he's been catching up to me a lot easier lately.

BRENDA
Maybe he's running faster.

MARGIE
No, I'm running slower. I guarantee it.

Margie smiles and winks, and Brenda finally gets it.

BRENDA
Ooooooh!

END

HANGING AT THE MALL

PENNY and JULIE are standing in the mall, talking.

PENNY

Hey, Julie, you with your mom or your dad this week?

JULIE

My dad.

PENNY

Wow. He's never let you come with us to the mall before, has he?

JULIE

Nope. Normally, he never lets me go.

PENNY

Why do you think he's so strict?

JULIE

He says it's because he loves me and is worried about me being around all
those strangers at the mall.

PENNY

Yeah, but you're with friends.

JULIE

I know. And he knows.

PENNY

So, how did you convince him to let you come this time?

JULIE

I had to agree to something. See that guy over there in the hat and
sunglasses?

PENNY

Yeah.

JULIE

That's my dad.

They both start laughing, and walk off.

END

FASHION
RACHEL and OLIVIA are on the patio, having tea, talking rather snooty.

RACHEL
Olivia, what do you think of my new dress?

OLIVIA
Um, it's nice, I suppose. I mean, it's not quite as nice as mine.

RACHEL
Well, you should know that purple is the new green. Or something like that.

OLIVIA
I can never keep up with all that fashion stuff.

RACHEL
Well, I like to stay in touch with the fashion world. It says so much about who you are in society.

OLIVIA
Well, it sounds a bit stuffy to me, my dear Rachel.

RACHEL
Well, my dear Olivia, now that you mention it, I tend to agree with you.

OLIVIA
That is a rather nice looking tree out back, don't you think?

RACHEL
I do, I do. Shall we get rid of these dresses, put on our jeans and go climb that tree, my dear Olivia?

OLIVIA
We shall, we shall, indeed, my dear Rachel.

They both jump up and run off, laughing.

END

ICE CREAM SCHEME

JOE and QUINN are talking in the back of the class.

JOE

Quinn, I have a plan to get us some ice cream.

QUINN

Okay, Joe, whatever it is, I'm in!

JOE

Here's the deal. You tell the teacher your stomach hurts, and you need to go see the school nurse. When she says yes, tell her you're too weak to go by yourself, and that I need to help you.

QUINN

How does that get us ice cream?

JOE

I'll tell the school nurse that it's appendicitis, and that ice cream will cure it. Then you can share your ice cream with me.

QUINN

Wait, my sister had appendicitis, and she didn't get ice cream, she got an operation!

JOE

That's because she's a girl. You're a guy. They'll give you ice cream. That's how it works.

QUINN

I don't believe you.

JOE

Hey, I'm just trying to get out of class for a few hours.

QUINN

Oh, brother. Thanks a lot. Okay. Teacher! Joe's stomach hurts!

JOE

What? No!

END

BUSTER FUZZY-MITTENS

ZOEY and ANNIE are talking before school.

ZOEY

I was so scared, Annie. I got home late from school yesterday, and Buster Fuzzy-Mittens was gone.

ANNIE

Oh, no. What did you do?

ZOEY

I looked everywhere, I ran down the street calling his name, I even looked in other people's back yards.

ANNIE

And then?

ZOEY

Then I went home, ran into my room, laid down on the bed, and started crying.

ANNIE

That's terrible! Did you ever find him?

ZOEY

Yes! I was crying, and Buster jumped up on the bed and laid down next to me to comfort me. He's such a good boy!

ANNIE

Where had he been?

ZOEY

He was hiding under my bed the whole time. Today, I'm going straight home from school so he won't be mad at me and hide again.

ANNIE

Zoey, you're pretty lucky to have a cool cat like Buster Fuzzy-Mittens!

ZOEY

I sure am, Annie. We're lucky to have each other.

END

PROUD FATHER

RUDY and STAN are talking before school.

RUDY
I am so depressed, Stan.

STAN
Why? What's wrong, Rudy?

RUDY
I just found out, I'm going to be a father.

STAN
What? How? Huh?

RUDY
My parents told me we're getting a new baby boy in a few months.

STAN
And you're the father?

RUDY
Well, yeah. My father's older than me, and he's my father. I'll be older than the new baby boy, so I'll be his father. That's how it works, right?

STAN
Um, I don't think so. I think you'll be his older brother.

RUDY
So I'm going to have a baby brother? Cool!

STAN
Feel better now?

RUDY
Yeah, except, well, now I'm not going to be a proud father.

STAN
(patting Rudy on the back)
Someday, Rudy. Someday.

END

A WHOOPING

BART and MICHAEL are talking on the playground.

BART

My mom got so mad at me the other day for pulling Alice's hair, she didn't even whoop me.

MICHAEL

No? What did she do?

BART

She told me she was going to tell my dad when he got home, and that he'd take care of it.

MICHAEL

That's terrible. How bad was it?

BART

Well, he grabbed a belt and took me in his office and closed the door. He said, "You know what you did was wrong, correct?" And I said, "Yes." He said, "Are you going to do it again?" And I said, "No."

MICHAEL

What happened next? Did he give you a whooping?

BART

He said, "Start yelling." He grabbed a book, and started hitting the book with the belt. I yelled, "Ow, ow, ow!" We both tried hard not to laugh.

MICHAEL

So, you never got a whooping for pulling Alice's hair?

BART

Nope. I think my mom bought it.

MICHAEL

You gonna do it again, then?

BART

Nope. I think that was my one freebie. Not taking the chance.

END

IN THE TREE
DENNIS and PATTI are standing under a tree, looking up.

DENNIS
Patti, do you think you could help me with something?

PATTI
With what?

DENNIS
My baseball glove is stuck in the tree.

PATTI
What's your baseball glove doing in the tree?

DENNIS
I threw it up there trying to knock my softball down.

PATTI
What was your softball doing up there?

DENNIS
I threw it up there trying to knock my Frisbee down.

PATTI
How'd your Frisbee get up there?

DENNIS
I tried to throw it over the roof, and the wind took it the other way and landed it in the tree.

PATTI
You know what, Dennis? You don't need help getting stuff down. You need help learning how to throw stuff.

DENNIS
Sadly, you may be right, Patti. You just may be right.

END

MOVING AWAY

ASHLEY and BRIAN are talking on Brian's front porch.

ASHLEY
I'm going away.

BRIAN
Where?

ASHLEY
Chicago.

BRIAN
For how long?

ASHLEY
Forever.

BRIAN
What? No! You can't! You're my best friend! What happened?

ASHLEY
My dad got a job there and we're moving there next week. I'm sorry.

BRIAN
What am I supposed to do without you here? Who's gonna help me with
my science homework? Who's gonna walk with me to the mall? Who's
gonna...who's gonna...

ASHLEY
You'll find someone else. We'll still be friends. We just can't see each
other. We can chat online, right?

BRIAN
It's not the same. I want you here, Ashley.

ASHLEY
I know, Brian. I'll miss you.

Ashley kisses Brian on the cheek and walks away.

BRIAN
Me, too.
END

BAD NEWS

QUINT and JAKE are in the parking lot near a baseball field.

QUINT

Jake, I have some bad news. The guys don't want you on the team anymore.

JAKE

You guys are dropping me? Why?

QUINT

You've hit one single all year, and struck out the rest of the time. Let's face it. You're not the best hitter on the team. Or the best pitcher. Or fielder.

JAKE

Yeah, Quint, but I'm not the worst, either. What about that little guy, Arnold?

QUINT

Yeah, he's not the greatest, but he does try hard.

JAKE

Try hard? He hasn't had a hit at all. And he always runs from the ball when you throw it at him.

QUINT

Yeah, but there's one very important thing you're missing.

JAKE
What?

QUINT

His dad always buys the pizza.

JAKE

Okay. I see your point. Can I still hang out with you guys after the game?

QUINT

Sure. There's always enough pizza to go around.

END

SPLITTING LUNCH

KIRA and STANLEY are seated in the school lunch room.

KIRA
I'll trade you my peanut butter sandwich for your potato chips.

STANLEY
No. These are ruffled. I don't get ruffled potato chips very often.

KIRA
But how often do you get peanut butter with banana?

STANLEY
No way! You got peanut butter with banana?

KIRA
Yup.

STANLEY
Wow. Tough decision.

KIRA
How about we split everything? I'll give you half my sandwich, and you give me half your chips and one of your cookies.

STANLEY
Hey! I've only got two cookies!

KIRA
That's what splitting is, silly!

STANLEY
Okay, I guess that's fair.

KIRA
And your pudding cup. Yoink!

Kira swipes the pudding cup. Stanley shakes his head.

END

NINJA ATTACK

DEANNA runs up to LIAM, who is sitting on the sidewalk, next to his bicycle, and his knee is scraped and bleeding.

DEANNA
Liam, are you okay?

LIAM
No, I don't think so.

DEANNA
Your knee is bleeding.

LIAM
Yeah. It was terrible, Deanna. This man stole a lady's purse, and I was chasing him on my bike--

DEANNA
Oh, my! You were chasing him?

LIAM
Yeah. I was gonna run him down and get the lady's purse back--

DEANNA
You are so brave.

LIAM
When out of the corner of my eye, I saw a Ninja come jumping out of the tree. He attacked me and knocked me off my bike. I was going to run after him, but he took off too fast.

DEANNA
Wow, you must be the bravest boy I know!

LIAM
Yeah. Did, um, you see any of that?

DEANNA
(smiling big)
No. But I did see my black cat *Midnight* run past the tree and scare you off your bicycle.

Liam face palms. Deanna walks away laughing.
END

AUDITION DAY

CLARICE and BONNIE are in the audition waiting room.

CLARICE
You ready for the big audition today, Bonnie?

BONNIE
Yeah, I guess so.

CLARICE
It's got to be pretty scary for you, being so new to the theatre, all this competition, standing in front of the director.

BONNIE
I'm not really that scared, Clarice.

CLARICE
Oh, you should be. It gets rough in there.

BONNIE
Rough?

CLARICE
Yeah. They shine these big spotlights on you, aim the camera and the microphone at you, and they make you say your lines six different ways.

BONNIE
Six different ways?

CLARICE
And then the director yells that you got it wrong every time.

BONNIE
That's too scary for me. I'm out.

Bonnie jumps up and runs away. Clarice smiles big.

CLARICE
Of course, it helps to reduce the competition. I'm ready for my close-up, Mr. DeMille!

END

CHRISTMAS WISH

Siblings SAM and PAT are sitting under the Christmas tree.

PAT

Hey, Sam. Did you get everything you wanted for Christmas this year?

SAM

Actually, no. Do you remember that girl we saw at the mall who asked Santa for no gifts? The one who said all she wanted for Christmas was to make up with her old best friend?

PAT

Yes. I remember her. That was pretty sad. What's that got to do with you?

SAM

Her name was Angela. And I know she didn't get what she asked for, because I'm the old best friend she was talking about. We argued about something stupid a while back. I can't even remember what it was now. And we haven't talked to each other since.

PAT

Sam, do you want your old best friend back?

SAM

Yes, Pat. Yes, I do.

PAT

Well, Sam. Then it's up to you to talk to her and make up.

SAM

You're right. Next time I see her I'm apologizing and giving her a big hug.

PAT

There you go. And don't go arguing about silly stuff anymore. Merry Christmas, Sam.

SAM

I won't. I promise. Nothing's worth losing your best friend over. Merry Christmas, Pat.

END

GIRLS PLAYING FOOTBALL

KARA and LANIE are talking on their way home from school.

LANIE
Kara, guess what?

KARA
What?

LANIE
Mrs. Mason is starting up a football team for the girls in our class.

KARA
Really? Cool! Who's gonna be on the team?

LANIE
Any girl that wants to.

KARA
Sweet! I'd love to sign up for that. Hey, Lanie.

LANIE
What?

KARA
What about cheerleaders?

LANIE
Cheerleaders? Seriously? You want to be a cheerleader?

KARA
No, silly. If the girls are playing football, I think we should have boy
cheerleaders.

LANIE
Why would you care about that?

KARA
I don't. I just want to see Justin running around in a skirt and waving his
pom-poms.

LANIE
Now that would be funny. I'll go sign him up right now!
END

SUPER-UNICORN

SUMMER and CHASE are in their front yard with their dog.

SUMMER
Sparks is a Super-Unicorn hero dog.

CHASE
Summer, Sparks is a dog with a paper towel tube tied to his head.

SUMMER
Shhhh... He doesn't know that.

CHASE
He doesn't know anything. He's a dog. And besides, there aren't any unicorns.

SUMMER
Chase, Sparks is a dreamer. He's powerful and strong. He's one of a kind. He sees himself as much more than just a dog. He's our protector. He's a hero.

CHASE
Do you really think he thinks that?

SUMMER
I do. Have you seen him growl when a stranger gets near us? Have you seen how he keeps watch while we're sleeping?

CHASE
Yeah, I guess I have.

SUMMER
That's because he knows that we're his family, and he'll protect us from all the bad stuff.

CHASE
You know, I think I get it. He's a proud dog, isn't he?

SUMMER
He's a proud Super-Unicorn hero dog.

END

SECRET AGENTS

JAMES and PENNY are hiding around the corner from the kitchen.

JAMES
Penny, have you confirmed target?

PENNY
James, intel has it that target is nearly ready for acquisition.

JAMES
Penny, what does nearly ready for acquisition mean?

PENNY
It means almost ready for us to take.

JAMES
Good, Penny. Just say that next time.

PENNY
Got it. I've read the file, and the timing should be right.

JAMES
We've got to be sure.

PENNY
I'm as sure as I can be. I know this is a critical mission.

JAMES
I trust you, Penny. I'm going in.
(reaching up and grabbing hot cookies, burning his fingers)
Ow! Target is hot! I repeat, target is hot! Mom just took the cookies out of the oven!

PENNY
Maybe I read the wrong recipe, I mean, file.

JAMES
You think next time we can just wait for mom to give us the cookies?

PENNY
I said the mission was critical, James. I was hungry for cookies *now*!

END

HAMBURGER SEEDS

JACK and EMILY are eating. Jack is plucking the seeds from his hamburger bun.

EMILY
Jack, what are you doing?

JACK
Gathering seeds.

EMILY
For what?

JACK
For my garden, silly.

EMILY
What are you planning to do with them?

JACK
I'm going to plant them, Emily.

EMILY
What do you think will grow?

JACK
Hamburgers. They're hamburger seeds. And when they grow, we can go to the garden and have hamburgers any time we want.

EMILY
But, Jack. Those are sesame seeds.

JACK
So, we'll have sesame hamburgers. I just hope the birds don't eat them.

EMILY
What birds?

JACK
The birds I'm growing with the bird seeds I planted last week.

EMILY
I don't think that will be a problem.
END

AUNTIE KISSES

DAVE and JOHN are sitting on the swings in the park.

JOHN
I hate it when we have parties at my house.

DAVE
Really? Why? Parties are supposed to be fun.

JOHN
Yeah, but my parents always invite the relatives, and they all pinch my cheeks and tell me how much I've grown. It's embarrassing. And my cheeks hurt. But the worst part is when my grandmother shows up. She keeps kissing me all over my face. And she's always tugging my ears and calling me her little munchkin.

DAVE
Ew. Grandma kisses. Yuck.

JOHN
But then there's my Auntie Kate.

DAVE
What horrible things does she do?

JOHN
It's not horrible. She kisses me on the nose and calls me her little cutie. And she smells nice.

DAVE
You like that?

JOHN
Have you seen my Auntie Kate?

DAVE
No.

JOHN
She's the cutie!

END

GET OFF MY LAWN

BONNIE and DARA are standing on the sidewalk.

DARA
Are you scared, Bonnie?

BONNIE
No. I mean, well, not really.

DARA
So, what are you waiting for?

BONNIE
If you're so brave, you do it.

DARA
It's your Frisbee.

BONNIE
You threw it.

DARA
You missed it

BONNIE
You threw it too hard.

DARA
Look, that house really isn't haunted. There is no ghost of an old man that grabs you if you walk on his lawn. That's just an old fairy tale. It's not real.

BONNIE
Fine. Here I go.

Bonnie steps forward onto the lawn to get her Frisbee. Dara yells out in a deep, scary voice.

DARA
Get of my lawn! Oooooooohhhhh!

Bonnie runs screaming. Dara laughs hysterically.

END

MODERN DESIGN

Siblings LUKE and LEAH are standing under a tree in their back yard.

LEAH

Of course it'll work, Luke. You just have to design it that way in the plans.

LUKE
What plans?

LEAH

You have to have plans when you're building anything. Otherwise, you won't know how to go about it.

LUKE

That's ridiculous. You just get all the stuff and build it. Design as you go.

LEAH

But how would you know what materials you need if you don't design a plan?

LUKE

You use whatever you can get. Stuff from the wood shed, leftover building materials from Eddie's dad's garage, and whatever nails and screws we can get from grandpa.

LEAH

I'm telling you, Luke, it's just going to be a disaster. And it won't be safe.

LUKE

It'll be fine if you just let me build it the way I want to build it.

LEAH

But the way you want to build it doesn't include a shoe closet.

LUKE

It's not supposed to have a shoe closet. It's a treehouse for us guys.

LEAH

Mom said you have to let me help and share it with me and my friends.

LUKE

This is going to be the worst treehouse ever!

END

TWO BOYS AND A WALLET
CALVIN and HOBBS have found a wallet on the street.

CALVIN
Hobbs, this wallet is full of money!

HOBBS
Finders keepers?

CALVIN
No, it's not ours.

HOBBS
Maybe the owner threw it away. Or maybe they're rich, and left it for someone who isn't rich to find it and keep it. Like us.

CALVIN
Maybe they lost it and really need it. What if this is all the money they have?

HOBBS
Then they should have taken better care of it, Calvin.

CALVIN
How would you like it if you lost something, really wanted it back, and whoever found it decided to keep it for themselves?

HOBBS
That would be crummy.

CALVIN
So, you see, we need to get this back to the rightful owner.

HOBBS
Maybe they'll give us a reward.

CALVIN
Maybe they'll be happy to get it back, and feeling good about returning it will be enough for us.

HOBBS
Yeah, you're right. You're a good guy, Calvin. If I ever lose anything, I hope you're the one who finds it.
END

SAFE HAVEN

JANET and CHRISSY are sitting at a lunch table at school.

JANET
Chrissy, why do you let those girls pick on you like that?

CHRISSY
What choice do I have, Janet?

JANET
You could stand up for yourself.

CHRISSY
They're bullies, there's a group of them, and they're all bigger than me.

JANET
So why don't you have a group of your own?

CHRISSY
Nobody wants me in their group.

JANET
How do you know? Have you asked anyone?

CHRISSY
Who would have me in their group?

JANET
Why would you say something like that?

CHRISSY
I'm not popular. I'm not cool. I don't dress cool like them.

JANET
Well, never mind them. I think you're plenty cool. If they pick on you again, or if you just feel like it, you can hang out with me and my friends any time you want.

CHRISSY
Thanks, Janet. You know, I think you're the cool one.

JANET
Anything for a new friend, Chrissy.
END

BIGFOOT

HENDERSON and HARRY are hiding behind a tree in Harry's back yard.

HENDERSON
Harry, how long do we have to wait here?

HARRY
As long as it takes, Henderson. This could be the find of the century.

HENDERSON
You don't really believe Bigfoot exists, do you?

HARRY
It's not for me to believe. It's for us, as scientists, to discover.

HENDERSON
Harry, we're not scientists.

HARRY
But we will be, if we can get evidence of a real Bigfoot.

HENDERSON
So, what makes you think he's around here?

HARRY
Last night, I heard noises around the garage. From my bedroom, I heard twigs breaking in the woods next door, and in the morning I found our garbage cans tipped over.

HENDERSON
And you think it was Bigfoot?

HARRY
What else could it be? Hey, did you hear that?

They both crouch down as they hear noises from the side of the garage. Henderson looks through his binoculars.

HENDERSON
Harry, unless Bigfoot is a raccoon, I think this was a waste of time.

HARRY
Okay. We can watch the pool tomorrow for the Loch Ness Monster.
END

CLOUDS

SABRINA and JAYDEN are lying back, looking at the clouds in the sky.

JAYDEN
What do you see, Sabrina?

SABRINA
I see a poodle. He's got a funny haircut and a poufy tail. What do you see?

JAYDEN
I see a monster truck, driven by a monster.

SABRINA
Look over there. There's Abraham Lincoln, but with a longer beard.

JAYDEN
No, I think it's Colonel Sanders. And there's a chicken.

SABRINA
Jeez. Do you see anything serious?

JAYDEN
Yes. A boy and a girl, about to hold hands.

SABRINA
You do? Where?

JAYDEN
Um, right here? Maybe?

SABRINA
Jayden?

JAYDEN
Yes, Sabrina?

SABRINA
I don't see that. Look for something serious.

JAYDEN
Can't blame a guy for trying! Look, Bigfoot!

END

THREE POINTER
CONNER and DENNY are on the basketball court.

DENNY
Swish! Three pointer! Nothing but net!

CONNER
That wasn't a three pointer, Denny. You were way over the line.

DENNY
No way, Conner. I was behind the line.

CONNER
How would you know? You weren't looking at the floor, you were watching the basket.

DENNY
Yeah, I was watching the ball swish right in.

CONNER
You were watching a lucky two pointer.

DENNY
Hey, I looked down right before I threw the ball. My feet were way behind the line.

CONNER
Yes, you're right. They were.

DENNY
See? I told you.

CONNER
That line. The three point line is back there, behind you.

DENNY
Seriously?

CONNER
Yup. Two pointer.

DENNY
Swish! Two pointer! Nothing but net!
END

DANCE OFF

PATTY and MARLENE are on the dance floor, out of breath.

PATTY
Marlene, I think I won that dance round.

MARLENE
Patty, you can't be serious. It wasn't even close.

PATTY
My triple moo cow was way better than your big parrot.

MARLENE
It's not a moo cow, it's called a Salchow, and that's a skating move.

PATTY
See how I bring new things to dancing?

MARLENE
You didn't even do that. And it's a pirouette, not a big parrot.

PATTY
My arms were out when I did mine because they were my wings. Mine
was a blue parrot.

MARLENE
That was not a pirouette or a blue parrot. It was just spinning.

PATTY
But I spun better than you did.

MARLENE
That's all you did. I was dancing. You just kept spinning and spinning.

PATTY
You call it spinning, I call it dancing. I won that round.
(grabbing her head with both hands.)
I think I need to sit down. All this dancing has got me dizzy.

MARLENE
Yup. Spinning.

END

THE GOOD LIE

OWEN and WILSON are sitting on the curb.

OWEN
Wilson, is there such a thing as a good lie?

WILSON
I don't know. I never thought about it, Owen.

OWEN
My parents always told me never to lie, because it was bad.

WILSON
Mine, too.

OWEN
I heard my dad talking on the phone the other day, and he kept talking about bad lies.

WILSON
He was?

OWEN
Yup. And if there are bad lies, I figure there must be good lies, too. Otherwise, they'd just be called lies.

WILSON
Sounds right to me. Who was he talking to?

OWEN
One of his golf buddies, I think.

WILSON
Did you ever figure out what he was talking about?

OWEN
No, but after he got off the phone, he told my mom he shot way under par.

WILSON
What's that mean?

OWEN
I don't know, but from the look on her face, I think that was a bad lie.
END

SHERLOCK AND HOLMES

SHERLOCK and HOLMES are investigating a strange animal in Holmes's house.

HOLMES
Sherlock, what do you make of this?

SHERLOCK
I'm not quite sure, Holmes. Looks like a Sphynx. Sphynx with a 'y', that is. It's pronounced 'sfinks'.

HOLMES
What's a Sphynx?

SHERLOCK
Well, Sphinx, spelled with an 'i', refers to The Great Sphinx of Giza, a large statue in Egypt.

HOLMES
And this one?

SHERLOCK
What I'm referring to here, is Sphynx with a 'y', which is a variety of domestic cat.

HOLMES
That's a cat? It looks weird. Where did it come from?

SHERLOCK
I believe a bit of investigation may provide a clue.

Sherlock gets down on his knees and looks through a magnifying glass.

HOLMES
What do you see, Sherlock?

SHERLOCK
Well, Holmes, I am deducing, based on the hair I see on the floor, and your little sister's hair trimmer she left behind, that your little sister was playing barber with your cat.

HOLMES
My cat? Fluffy? Fluffy! Noooooooooooo!
END

SKI LIFT

ANGIE and MARCIE are sitting in a ski lodge, drinking hot cocoa.

ANGIE
Marcie, how was your day on the slopes?

MARCIE
Dreadful, Angie. Absolutely dreadful. I started off on the bunny hill. And I was doing really well.

ANGIE
And?

MARCIE
And I went down the bunny hill a few times, and held onto that rope to get back to the top. Then I saw all these people sitting on this ski lift, and I thought, "Why do I keep grabbing the rope when I can just ride back up?" So I got on it. And it took me past the bunny hill and all the way up to the top of the mountain!

ANGIE
How exciting! Did you get to ski from the top all the way down?

MARCIE
Actually, I was afraid to, so I stayed on the ski lift so it would take me back down. But once I was down there, I was embarrassed to get off, because it would look like I chickened out.

ANGIE
So what did you do?

MARCIE
I just kept riding the lift until one of the workers saw me and pulled me off.

ANGIE
That had to be embarrassing. It does sound like you had a dreadful day.

MARCIE
Yeah, but it's over now. And I've got hot cocoa and good company. This turned out to be a good day, after all. I'm coming back next weekend. Wanna come?

END

PIE, GLORIOUS PIE

Siblings OLIVER and NANCY are on the back porch. Oliver is lying on a bench, moaning.

OLIVER
I think I'm dying, Nancy.

NANCY
Should I get mom and dad?

OLIVER
No! I mean, um, no. I'd rather die peacefully, alone, on this bench, on our back porch.

NANCY
Oliver, what happened?

OLIVER
I think I'm allergic to apples.

NANCY
What makes you think that?

OLIVER
I ate some, and now my stomach feels like it's going to explode.

NANCY
Where did you get the apples from?

OLIVER
The apple pie mom made.

NANCY
Mom made apple pie? Where is it? I want some.

OLIVER
There isn't any. I ate it all.

NANCY
You ate the whole pie? You're not allergic. You're a piggy!

OLIVER
I need some cake. That would make me feel better.
END

REPLACED

Siblings MICHELLE and JORDAN are sitting on the schoolyard swings.

JORDAN
Tell me what's wrong, little sis. You look depressed.

MICHELLE
Mom and Dad don't love me any more, Jordan.

JORDAN
Why would you say that?

MICHELLE
They're replacing me. I heard them say we're getting a new baby sister.
I'm the baby sister.

JORDAN
You're *my* baby sister. This one will be a baby sister for both of us.

MICHELLE
But I don't want a baby sister. I want you to have me all to yourself.

JORDAN
Well, Michelle, you know how I play with you, help you climb trees, help
you down when you get stuck, cover for you when Mom and Dad are mad,
and teach you things like bike riding and swimming?

MICHELLE
Yeah.

JORDAN
Well, I really enjoy doing those things for you, Michelle. And soon you'll
be able to enjoy doing those things, too. And you'll be the big sister.

MICHELLE
Jordan, will you still be my big brother?

JORDAN
Always, peanut.

MICHELLE
Then I guess I don't mind so much getting a new baby sister. I'm not being
replaced, I'm getting promoted.
END

ALMOST BUSTED

BEN and ELI are in a video game store.

ELI
Ben, don't do it, man.

BEN
I'm not doing anything, Eli.

ELI
I saw you. You put that video game in your shirt. You're trying to steal it, and not only is that wrong, you could get busted for it.

BEN
Hey, I've spent lots of money here. They owe me one. Besides, if they catch me, I'll put it back.

ELI
If they catch you, it'll be too late. They'll call the police, the police will call your parents, and you'll have an arrest record. You'll be in way more trouble than that game is worth.

BEN
Naw. I'll just walk right out that door, and they won't know a thing.

ELI
Yes, they will. Because I'll tell them before you leave the store.

BEN
You'd squeal on me? Why would you do that? I thought you were my friend.

ELI
I *am* your friend. That's why I would tell. I'd rather see them tell you to put it back now, than to have them call the police on you after you leave the store with it. That's what real friends do.

BEN
So, you're just looking out for me? Okay, I'm putting it back. Thanks for being a real friend, Eli.

ELI
Thanks for seeing things my way, friend.
END

FUNNIEST VIDEO
MARCY and DARCY are at the computer.

DARCY
Marcy, that was the funniest cat video, ever. I can't wait to get it on
YouTube. It'll go viral in a day, I'm sure.

MARCY
We'll be world famous, Darcy. I can see it now, "The Marcy and Darcy
team that filmed the crazy cat that jumped in the dishwater, freaked out,
and ran all over the house."

DARCY
Yeah. The Darcy and Marcy team.

MARCY
Either way. Hey, pull it up and we'll watch it again before putting it online.

Darcy clicks, and they both watch in horror.

MARCY
Oh, no! That's not the cat. That's my brother making faces in the camera.

DARCY
Look, he's holding up a sign. It says, "I replaced your stupid cat video with
this! Ha, ha."

MARCY
That little monster!

DARCY
Our crazy cat video is gone. What are we going to do?

MARCY
I'll tell you what we're going to do. We'll post this video instead. We'll
call it, "Crazy little brother makes stupid faces in the camera." It'll go
viral, for sure.

DARCY
You're a genius, Marcy!

MARCY
I am indeed, Darcy. I am indeed.
END

74

GOT GLUE?

WYATT and BILLY are picking up pieces of a broken vase in the house.

BILLY
That was some mighty fine shooting there, Wyatt.

WYATT
Not too bad yourself there, Billy.

BILLY
However, now that we've busted up the town, we've got some cleaning up
to do.

WYATT
I just wonder how we're going to explain this one to the mayor.

BILLY
You mean, your mom?

WYATT
Yeah. That was her favorite vase.

BILLY
Maybe we could tell her the cat did it. Or the dog.

WYATT
We don't have a cat, Billy. Or a dog.

BILLY
Got any glue?

WYATT
Yes. Glue, we have.

BILLY
You think we'll be able to glue the vase back together so she won't know?

WYATT
Nope. We're going down. The mayor is gonna lock us up for sure.

BILLY
It's been good shooting with you, Wyatt. I think I hear my mom calling.
Bye!
END

IMPRACTICAL JOKE
Siblings MEGAN and CAMERON are hiding in the bushes.

CAMERON
Megan, I can't wait to see the look on Mom's face when she opens the mailbox.

MEGAN
Me, either, Cameron. It's gonna be so funny.

CAMERON
Yeah, when she pulls it open and that spring loaded snake comes flying out, she's gonna scream so loud!

MEGAN
I know. And just think how funny it's going to be when she reads the note.

CAMERON
I know. That'll be so...wait...what note?

MEGAN
The note that says, "Hey, Mom. Hope you like your surprise. Cameron."

CAMERON
I didn't put a note in there.

MEGAN
I know. That part was my idea. I put it in there. Like it?

CAMERON
Why would you do something like that?

MEGAN
I figured, as long as we're setting up practical jokes, why not make it a double?

CAMERON
Oh, no! She's headed to the mailbox! Mom! Wait!

Cameron runs to stop his mom, but is too late. His mom screams.
Megan laughs runs in the other direction.

END

BACKYARD THEME PARK

MICKEY and MINNIE are in their back yard.

MINNIE

Hey, Mickey. I'm glad we decided to open our own theme park.

MICKEY

I know, Minnie. This is going to be so much fun.

MINNIE

Did you get the balloons?

MICKEY

Yup. A big bag. You just have to blow them up now. Here you go.

MINNIE

Why do I have to blow them up?

MICKEY

We said we'd split everything fifty-fifty, right? I got the balloons, you blow them up.

MINNIE

That's not fair. I don't have that much air in me. You have to help.

MICKEY

I'll be busy with the hose, filling up the duck pond for Daffy and Donald.

MINNIE

Don't make me go all Tasmanian Devil on you!

MICKEY

Oh, don't be an Ani-Maniac.

MINNIE
(stomping off)
That's it! I quit!

MICKEY

Now you're just being Goofy!

MINNIE
I heard that!
END

ALIEN ABDUCTION
Siblings ELLIOTT and GERTIE are hiding in the tool shed.

GERTIE
Elliott, what are we doing out here in the tool shed?

ELLIOTT
Waiting. We're waiting, Gertie. Waiting and watching.

GERTIE
For what?

ELLIOTT
For aliens.

GERTIE
From outer space?

ELLIOTT
Yes. Shush. I think I just heard one mumble.

GERTIE
That was my stomach. I'm hungry.

ELLIOTT
You just had dinner a couple of hours ago.

GERTIE
Hey, didn't Mom give you two bags of candy for us to eat?

ELLIOTT
Yes. Now be quiet. The aliens could be here at any moment.

GERTIE
Where's my candy?

ELLIOTT
I used it as bait. The aliens ate it. Both bags.

GERTIE
Then why do you have all those empty wrappers in your pocket? Hey! You
ate the all the candy! And you said the aliens ate it all. That
means...Mooooommmmmm! Elliott's an alien!
END

UNMASKED AVENGER

Friends BRUCE and WAYNE are hiding by the side of Bruce's house.

WAYNE

Bruce, I don't think we should go out after the street lights are on. It could be dangerous.

BRUCE

Wayne, danger is what I do. Danger is my middle name.

WAYNE

No, it's not. It's Edward. Your mom told me.

BRUCE

Today, my trusty sidekick, it's Danger. And we are about to rid this city of all its villains. We will go into the night and do what we, as superheroes, must do. We will foil every last one of those crafty, evil doers.

WAYNE

Is that why you've got your sister's black makeup all around your eyes?

BRUCE

Yes, Wayne. It's my superhero disguise. No one must know the secret identity of me, Rocky Danger Raccoon, prowler of vengeance in the night, with his trusty sidekick, Rat Boy.

WAYNE

Bruce, you need to wash that off. Your sister's going to be mad you used all her makeup to play superheroes and villains.

BRUCE

She doesn't scare me. Her powers are nothing compared to mine.

WAYNE

I think I hear her coming.

BRUCE

Away, good Rat Boy, away! We'll live to fight another day!

Bruce runs away, wiping the makeup off his eyes. Wayne laughs at him.

END

MONOLOGUES FOR TEENS

STARGAZING

I sometimes look to the stars, hoping to get answers to all my questions. Even just some of them. That would be okay. But I'm finding that the more time passes, the more questions I have. There's something magical up there, I know it, but people keep telling me to stop stargazing. To keep my feet on the ground. To not reach further than my grasp. Yeah, maybe the answers aren't up there. Maybe I need to look inside more, try to figure out things for myself. But I do know there's wonder out there, and I'll never stop looking up.

BEING TEEN

Yeah, I know. I'm just a teenager. What could I know about life, huh? I'll tell you. I've been through more crap in my few years on this planet than most people your age could even imagine. You don't know the stress. Homework, sports, having your heart broken the day after prom. And trying to keep up with fashion? Trying to look cool all the time? You have no idea.

RUMORS

Mark knew how I felt about him. He knew there was no way I'd ever cheat on him. I loved him. Everybody knew that. And when Chad decided to make those things up about me, when he told those disgusting lies, I expected Mark to stand up to him. To stand up for me. To defend my honor. But did he? No! He believed Chad and dropped me like a rock. Do you have any idea how that made me feel? Then, a few days later, I see Mark and Chad hanging out in the park together. Laughing it up, having a good old time. It was all a setup. Mark wanted to break up with me, but didn't have the courage to tell me to my face, so he had Chad spread horrible rumors about me, all so Mark would have an excuse to dump me. Now my reputation is ruined, I'm alone, and Mark's moved on with some bimbo cheerleader. Well, good luck with him, honey. When you're no longer the flavor of the week, come see me, and we'll compare stories.

WHEN I WAS YOUR AGE

My dad always told me stories about when he was my age. All about "When I was your age, we didn't have video games," or, "When I was your age, we had to do chores before we could have our dinner," or "When I was your age," blah, blah, blah. I think when he was my age, he spent all his time writing down all the things he was going to tell his future kid about "When he was my age."

TOO QUIET

When I got home, something just didn't feel right. It was too quiet. My twin sister and my younger brother were usually arguing about something, with mom in the middle trying to break it up. I saw the small table in the entry hall had been knocked over and the vase that sat on it was in pieces on the floor. Since no one was yelling, blaming someone else, and nobody was sweeping it up, of course I imagined the worst. So I dialed 911. I called you guys. Right before you got here, my mother, brother, and sister pulled up. They'd been to the pet store, buying toys for the new puppy they adopted this morning. Apparently, this time, we can blame it on the dog.

HEAVY

Yeah, I'm a little overweight. Okay, a lot overweight. I have issues. Image issues, emotional issues, social issues. Maybe it's all the same, I don't know. I like food. A lot. I try to eat right. I try to eat smaller portions. I try to exercise when I can. It just doesn't seem to help. I'm sure genetics are involved somehow. My parents are both heavy. It doesn't seem to bother them. But they're not in high school. They don't have people laughing at them. Pointing. Making insults. I just want to be accepted for who I am. Someone who is just like everyone else, just...heavier. Part of me wishes I could be one of those thin cheerleaders. Part of me wants to go hide somewhere. Part of me thinks these other kids have to pick on me because they don't know any better, or because they're insecure and making fun of someone else makes them feel better about themselves. Maybe if I just get past high school and all these posers, I'll fit into society and be just fine. Maybe I just have to ignore them, and be happy with me, just the way I am.

MONOLOGUE ANGEL

So, there I was in acting class, going over my lines for my monologue. I looked up, and there she was, standing in front of the room, giving her monologue. She was an angel. Her deep blue eyes, her long, curly blonde hair, her petite, frail body all dressed in white, with that orange sash wrapped around her midriff. Her voice was so smooth and gentle, I was so wrapped up in the sound of her, that afterwards, I couldn't remember a single word she said. And when it was my turn to get in front of the class, I couldn't remember a single word of my monologue.

LUNCH MONEY

Not cool? It's not cool? Come one, dude, it's a joke. A prank. Me and Eric broke into your locker when you were in the shower. You weren't supposed to look in your wallet until lunch. We thought it'd be funny to see you freaking out, not being able to pay for your cheeseburger. Look, Eric's got your money, but I'll loan you a few bucks for lunch until he shows up. (Pulls wallet out, finds it to be empty) My wallet! It's empty! What are you laughing at? Not cool, dude. Not cool.

MUSIC MAN

I love the theatre. Especially musical theatre. The drama department was having auditions for The Music Man. The drama teacher said we should all try out. I jumped at the chance. Imagine me, on stage, playing Robert Preston's role, singing and dancing and romancing Marion the librarian. Personally, I thought I nailed the audition. The next day in drama class, the teacher was lecturing on the art of singing. She said that anyone can sing. Singing is nothing more than sustained talking. Yes, anyone can sing. Then she paused, walked to where I was sitting, and placed her hand on my shoulder. She looked at the rest of the class and said, "Well, almost anyone." No. I didn't get the role of Harold Hill. I was a pretty darned good stage hand, though. Best in River City.

MY FRIEND

My friend invited me to smoke some pot. When I told him I wasn't interested, he laughed at me. Said I was chicken. Said everyone was doing it. From what I could see, not everyone was doing it. The guys with lower grades in school, the ones spending money on something illegal, the ones putting themselves at risk of being arrested, having a criminal record, of having their parents spend thousands of dollars on legal fees. Yeah, those were the ones smoking pot. Hey, I don't have to agree with the law, but I'm going to abide by it. It's not worth the risk to my future. If that makes me chicken, then I guess I'm chicken. And my friend? If he wants to try and bully me into risking my future to do something stupid with him, then I guess he's not much of a friend, now is he?

MAKING IT BIG

One day, I'm going to make it big. I'm going to be on Jeopardy. I'm going to win more money than anybody has ever won on that show. People will look up to me. I'll get big companies endorsing me, I'll do commercials, maybe even get to play myself in a movie about me. My parents will be proud of me, my friends will all invite me to their parties, and all the girls will want to be with me. I'll be more popular than, than, I don't know. Someone really popular. Of course that means I'll have to study. A lot. I'll have to get my grades above a C minus. Or win the lottery. That could work. One day, I'm going to make it big. Really big.

FISHING

My mom and dad are both really great people, just, not together. I used to go fishing with my dad on the weekends. We'd get up early, hit the lake, fish from shore until about noon. Then we'd stop for pizza or chili dogs on the way home. That was before he got so busy working late nights and weekends at his office. My mom and I had an art class we were taking together on Tuesday nights. Then she started skipping out to hang out with her friends. She said they needed her support. I guess she thought I didn't. It turned out mom and dad both had other interests. They live in different houses now. I spend the week with my mom, helping her to redecorate. I'm with my dad on the weekends. We go fishing every now and then.

MONOLOGUE ADONIS

So, there I was in acting class, going over my lines for my monologue. I looked up, and there he was, standing in front of the room, giving his monologue. He was an Adonis. His deep blue eyes, his long, jet black hair, his perfectly masculine body, poured into those stonewash jeans, topped off with that tight V-neck t-shirt. His voice was so deep and smooth, I was so wrapped up in the sound of him, that afterwards, I couldn't remember a single word he said. And when it was my turn to get in front of the class, I couldn't remember a single word of my monologue.

INVISIBLE

No one sees me. Kids pass me in the halls without looking at me. Teachers don't notice when I raise my hand in class. It's like I'm invisible. I can deal with all that. But, Chris. Chris doesn't see me. That's the one that hurts the worst. She's sweet, kind, smart, pretty. Very pretty. Not Hollywood pretty. Better. Natural pretty. Like she would easily get lost in a crowd if you weren't looking for her. But I look through the crowd, and she's all I see. I stood at my locker the other day, waiting for everyone to pass so I could go to class without being bumped into, and I saw her down the hall, walking my way. She walked by, giving me an honest smile as she passed. And then she was gone. Maybe there's hope. Maybe I'm not that invisible after all.

NEWS REPORT

Hear it all right here. The teachers, the students, the neighbors, the family. All the news you want to hear, and some you don't. Mrs. Barker's cat stuck in a tree. Fire department saves the cat by cutting the tree down. Neighborhood man sues fire department for cutting down his favorite tree. Students at local high school rally to ban cats from climbing trees. Area animal shelter stands against students in favor of feline rights. Local news reporter grounded by his parents for spreading fake news reports. Yeah, that last one. That's me. This will be my last news report for at least two weeks. Until next time, this is Lane Edwards, signing off.

CLASS PET

Mr. Ide wrote a musical play when he was in college, and now he wants our drama class to perform it on stage for the whole school. I thought, of course he's got his class pets to play the main roles, so I'm not gonna get cast in it. Well, I got cast. I'm one of the lead characters. So, either I'm really good, or I'm one of his class pets. I'm hoping it's the former, and not the latter. I'd like to think I got cast because I'm that good. I'd hate to think I got the role because of all the cupcakes I brought him for lunch every day. Or the times I washed his car. Or...never mind.

PIECES

I've been trying to pick up the pieces for days. It's the miniature glass piano she bought me for my last birthday. It's everywhere. Even when I think I'm done, I keep finding pieces. I threw it against the wall. I know, it was a dumb thing to do, but I kind of lost it when she left. When you're that angry, you don't think at the time how much you're gonna miss something when it's gone, and you end up doing things you regret. But the pieces are still there. I think I'm gonna be finding them for a long time.

HAPPIEST MOMENT

Happiest moment of my life! She walked into the classroom, I took one look at her and bam! Yeah, bam! She was unbelievably hot! I sat up a little taller in my seat, hoping she'd notice me. She did. Oh, yeah. She strolled by, smiled, and sat right behind me. I didn't say anything right away. Had to play it cool, you know. About ten minutes later, she was poking me in the back with the eraser end of her pencil. Then her hand came around my arm. She handed me a note. I looked down and opened it real quick. It said, "Meet me at the library after school." Then she tapped my arm and whispered in my ear, "Hey, be a sweetheart and pass that to the guy in front of you." Yeah. Happiest moment of my life, over.

AVERAGE

I always thought Walter was a great guy. A little nerdy, a little different, but I never had a problem with him. The jocks always picked on him, made fun of him for not being overly coordinated. His grades weren't the best. Average, I guess. He was just an average guy. That doesn't make you a bad person, it just makes you average. I guess that's just not enough for some people. I guess some people just have to make themselves feel better by putting other people down. Some people are sensitive, take stuff like that to heart. Walter was one of those people. He found his dad's gun, and put an end to all of it. Now Walter's gone, and the people that made him feel inferior are still doing what they've always been doing, making themselves feel better by putting others down. Will any one of us learn from any of this? I hope so. I guess we'll just have to wait and see.

BASEBALL CARD

Did you really think I wasn't going to notice? You think I'm that stupid? You used my Hank Aaron baseball card as a coaster for your lemonade. Then you clothes-pinned it to your bicycle so you could make motor sounds riding down the street. Then it fell off, landed in the yard, and got run over with a lawn mower. You then taped the pieces back together, with duct tape! And now you're telling me my kid brother did it? No. He wouldn't do anything like this. He knows better. I'm sorry, I don't believe you, Mom.

HOW YOU FELT

If only I had known. You never told me you felt that way about me. Why didn't you say something, just give me a clue? I mean, I don't know what I would have said, what I would have done, but, at least, if I knew, maybe we could have…I don't know. But now…I'm going to the prom with Chris. Maybe we'll really hit it off. Maybe we'll stay together for a while. Maybe we'll settle down, get married, have kids, grow old and die together. Maybe…maybe that could have been you and me. All you had to do was tell me how you felt about me. Or, I guess, maybe I should have told you how I felt about you.

SINK OR SWIM

I can't believe I'm going to be on my own. All my life I've depended on my parents for food, clothes, a place to live. I get my first job, and they tell me to get out? Is this throwing me in the water to see if I can swim? If that's what it is, then fine. I'll swim. I'll work hard at my job, I'll get promoted, I'll get raises, I'll manage my finances, I'll pay my bills, and I'll make it on my own. I'll get an education, a career, a family of my own. If that's what they want, then I'll show them. I'll do it. I'll be a success…wow…um…yeah. Okay, I get it. Thanks, Mom and Dad.

COLLEGE

Um, okay. How do I say this? Here we go. You want me to get a business degree. I'm not going to college. I know that's not what you want to hear, but it's my decision to make. I just don't see the point in it. You guys spending tens of thousands of dollars, me working for the next four to eight years to learn something I may not even want to do anymore by the time I graduate, if there's even a need for my particular degree in the work force by then. I'd rather pursue my art, my music, my theatre, and see where those things take me. I think I've got talent. I just need to learn more about those things. Hey, wait, they have college courses in the arts, right? Okay, maybe we can talk college. Meet me in the middle?

STORIES

Oh, my goodness! This is awesome! You wrote this? You have got such an amazing imagination. Where do you come up with this stuff? If I could write one tenth as good as you do, I'd spend all my time writing. Seriously. You have a gift. To be able to tell stories, to paint pictures in people's minds the way you do, just, wow. I would never have imagined that someone your age, someone so young, would have had enough life experience to be able to pull a reader in the way you do. Oh, and one more thing…you forgot to delete the real author's name when you copied and pasted this chapter from his book. So, I guess there was a little truth in there somewhere. You are telling stories.

SECOND PLACE

Second place is not for me. It's first place or nothing. My dad always told me that, so I had to believe it. There's no place for losers in this world, and second place is just the first one to lose. That's what he told me. Over and over again. And the harder I work at it, the more I think, maybe he's right, maybe not. I mean, there's only so much room at the top, right? Someone has to be first, and when that spot is taken, is second really so bad? Maybe it's all right to not be first, if you've really tried your hardest, and someone else just happens to be better. Maybe it's okay to just be all you can be, and not worry about what everyone else is doing. It's not a cop out. I just think, if you really do try to do your honest best, that's all you can do, and you should be proud of yourself for that. Just be proud of me, Dad. I'm doing all I can, for both of us.

ALIBI

How could you put me in this situation? You break into a liquor store, steal a bunch of booze, and you want me to be your alibi? You want me to lie for you? Tell the police you were with me all night? I can't lie for you. Not to the police. What if they find more evidence and convict you? Then I go to jail for perjury. Or worse yet, they convict me for being your accomplice, because I said we were together all night. I thought you were my friend. Friends don't do this to each other. I'm sorry, but I can't. I can't lie for you. You can lay your guilt trip on me all you want, but I'm not the one asking a friend to risk his future over someone else's crime. I'm your friend, but I can't be your alibi. Not for this.

NEWFOUND RESPECT

There's this kid at school. Luke. He doesn't really talk much. I pass him in the hallway now and then, but he doesn't acknowledge me. Or anyone else, for that matter. We all figured that he was a tough guy, or was really shy, or just didn't like people. Nobody knew him well enough to say for sure. I saw him the other day at the grocery store. He didn't see me. There was an old man with a terrible disability standing in the aisle. He walked funny and his arms were twisted and his hands were balled up in fists. He was trying to get some larger items off the shelf to put in his cart, and was having a really hard time. Luke walked up to the man and pointed at what the man was trying to pick up. The old man nodded, and Luke picked it up and put it in the man's cart. Luke followed the man and helped him do the rest of his shopping. When the man got everything he needed, he gave Luke a hug, and Luke hugged him back. I now have a lot of respect for Luke. Sometimes, you just never know who you're looking at.

OLD SCHOOL

I moved here from the country. I was a big man at my old school. Everyone knew who I was. They knew I wasn't a bully, but they knew not to mess with me. They knew I stood up for the kids who couldn't defend themselves. They knew I hung around with the kids I liked, not the ones who would make me look popular. Most of them respected me for that. Here it's a different story. Whole different world. Everyone wants to be cool, popular, fit in. If you don't rebel, fight the system, skip class, hang with the gangs, then you're not normal. There's no respect here. Envy, fear, but no real respect. I miss my old school. I miss the respect.

SUPERPOWERS

My superpowers are basically a combination of all the superpowers from all the superheroes combined. So, in a fight, I of course would always be the winner. There are a few powers I'm missing…just the ones presently had exclusively by any supervillain. Considering, however, that the superhero always wins, things still average out in my favor. So, as you can see on my resume, I don't have much experience in the fast food industry, but hiring me would still be adding a great asset to your company.

LOOKING BACK

I'm not letting you bring me down. I've worked hard, I got good grades, I'm getting into a good college, and nothing you say can change that. You wanted me to skip out and party with you, hang out with your friends, and miss my education. I didn't do that, and now you're leaving me because in your mind that makes me a loser? Maybe I'm not good enough for you anymore, but I'm plenty good enough for the rest of the world. And one day, you'll look back and realize that you let go of the greatest thing that ever happened to you. And one day, I'll look back, and I'll know I lost you. And I'll miss you. But I won't be unappreciated.

MEATBALLS

I wanted Karl to take me out to dinner. No sitting at his place watching Disney movies like he always wants to do. Nothing special, just a night out together without everyone else hanging around being goofy. You know, nobody to influence Karl and make him do silly stuff to make them laugh. He took me to a nice little Italian restaurant around the corner. Just the two of us. It was really nice. We ordered spaghetti and meatballs. Soft music was playing. It was romantic. It was going really well, until he saw a couple of his buddies sitting a few tables over. Karl barked like a dog until he got everyone's attention, then pushed his meatball over to me with his nose. Disney romantic, with a big side of so embarrassing. That's Karl.

DRIVER TRAINING

Driving a car is a piece of cake. A few simple rules, a couple of gages to glance at, accelerator, brake. Not much to it, really. Of course the driving instructor seems to think it's rocket surgery. Hands at ten and two, eyes on the road, look in the mirror, look in the other mirror. Look in the mirror to see the traffic behind you, not to comb your hair. Slow down. Signal your turns. Signal your lane changes. Don't drive so close to the car in front of you. Don't make faces at the police officer. Hey, I'm doing fine. He should just pass me and let me get my driver's license. Look, my parents have been driving for twenty years, and everything I'm doing seems to have worked for them.

BESTSELLING AUTHOR

I'm going to be taking journalism classes when I get to college. Plan on graduating with honors and landing a job writing for one of the big publications. New York Times, probably. Do that for a few years, get some experience under my belt, then start writing novels. Make the bestseller list, travel around doing book signings, and retire somewhere warm. So, there's my beginning, middle, and end. I'll fill in all the spaces along the way. Yeah, I plan on it being quite the ride. When it's all over, I'll leave my notes behind and someone else can publish my memoir. Too bad I won't be around to read the book about my life. It's gonna be good. Real good.

PARTING SORROW

"No, Jane, darn it! You know I love you, but I just can't do this! Release me! Live your life! You're better off without me! You've got so much going for you. You don't need me dragging you down. Holding you back. I know it'll be tough for you, but you're strong. You'll get through this. Someday, I'll barely be a memory to you. You'll live a good life, and I'll be happy for you. Good-bye, my darling." That's what I was going to say to her, right before she dumped me like a ton of cinder blocks. Good-bye, my darling.

PROM DATE

Everyone had a date for the prom. It was so nice. We'd all been concerned that the big day was coming, and none of us guys had dates, much less girlfriends. Then just a few weeks before prom, everything started coming together. Maybe because spring was in the air. Maybe we'd all just reached that age when we were looking for that special someone. Not soul mates or anything Earth shattering, just someone of the other gender that we could really enjoy being with. Someone to hold hands with while walking through the halls at school. We all had girlfriends. It felt good. Then about a week after prom, me and the guys were all sitting in my garage, discussing the whole thing. By then, none of us had girlfriends anymore. They had all broken up with us. We figured out that day, that apparently, every one of the girls in school thought it was pretty important to have a date for the prom, too.

SHIFTING GEARS

Okay, I might as well tell you, I guess. It's over. What's done is done. I was challenged to a drag race on my way home from my job at the mall the other day. One of the older girls I work with, she's in her twenties, pulled up to me at the light and revved her engine. I figured, let's do this. The light turned green and we took off. We were driving side by side, booking along pretty good, and I decided to rev my engine to look tough. So I shifted into neutral and hit the gas. Vroom! Thing is, I shifted too far and slammed it into reverse. She won, my transmission is shot, and I looked pretty pathetic trying to explain to my parents why I needed money to fix my car.

TEAM CHEER

Me and the girls went to the park yesterday. A bunch of the guys from school were playing football. We decided to be the cheerleaders, so we broke off pieces of a tree and used them as pom-poms. It turned out some of the player's girlfriends were there, and thought we were hitting on their boyfriends. We thought it was funny, so we cheered even harder, jumped up and down, waving our leaves, and kicking our legs like the Rockettes. The girlfriends got their own branches and started cheering, trying to outdo us. It turned into quite the competition. After an hour or so, we were all worn out and gave up. We looked, and the game was over, and all the guys had left to go get pizza. So we all got together, us and the girlfriends, and went to the mall for ice cream. Pretty good day, all in all.

GETTING HOME LATE

Mom, Dad, I know I'm late. Please don't blame Sam. It was all my fault. I wasn't watching the time. Sam was doing really well at the carnival games, the lines were short to get on the rides, and we were just having such a great time. And I know I missed dinner, but we had corn dogs and elephant ears and lemonade. I know that doesn't make for a great meal, but we just wanted to fill up before listening to the band play. When we noticed what time it was, Sam brought me straight home. Also, can I see Sam again tomorrow night? There's a great new movie playing at the theater. I promise I'll be home on time.

WHAT A DOLL

My dad took me to the mall the other day for an appointment with the optometrist. We were there early, so we sat in the mall next to the pretzel kiosk and ate pretzels until it was time for my exam. While we were sitting there, this really pretty girl kept staring at me through the window at the women's clothing store. She was smiling really sweet. What a doll. I was about to go in and introduce myself, when my dad said we had to go. An hour later, I had my new glasses, and went back to see if there was any chance she was still there. She was. Of course she was. I could see clearly now, she was a mannequin. Yeah, what a doll.

FASHION POLICE

No, this is not what I normally wear. Dress pants, dress shirt, tie. Not my thing. I look like my dad. I mean, not that it's a bad thing. He's successful, goes to work every day, and brings home a good paycheck. It's just not me. The clothes, I mean. So before you get all fashion police on me, just know that I'm normally a pretty modern dresser. I got a whole closet full of way cooler stuff than this. And yes, this is my first job interview, so I was told I needed to wear a tie for first impressions and all that stuff. I just wanted you to know, on a personal level, that I'm normally a really sharp dresser. Oh, you do? You want me to dress like this for work every day? Sure, no problem. I've got a whole closet full of dress shirts and ties.

WHO NEEDS BOYS?

Boys. Oh, boy. Do you think nature could have made anything more useless? They're either hanging out with each other, playing sports, playing video games, or getting into some kind of trouble. When you're younger, they pull your hair and run. When they get a little older, they want to copy your homework. After that, well, I'm still waiting to see. But whatever they do, I'm sure I'm not going to like that, either. My older sister has a boyfriend. He's around all the time. We can't get rid of him. He must be pretty far behind on his homework, I'll say that for sure.

BIGGER DREAMS

I had bigger dreams. I was going to go all the way. Was gonna make it to the top. I was the best player on the team. I was looking forward to getting offers from all the big franchises. Multi-million dollar contracts, buying a new home for my parents, being world famous, the whole deal. My friends knew I was going to make it, too. They all had faith in me. They decided to throw me an early celebration party. We all got together at Jim's parent's house while they were away and had a major blast. There was alcohol, and they wanted me to drink with them, but I refused. I wasn't going to let anything stand in the way of my career. A couple of the guys got drunk and thought it would be funny to tackle me on the living room floor when I wasn't looking, just so one day they could say that they took down the star athlete. We fell on the coffee table, my leg broke in three places, and my ankle was crushed. Yeah, they took me down, all right. I'll never be able to run like I could before. Now I work a cash register. I had bigger dreams.

COUNTRY MUSIC STAR

My parents bought me a guitar for my birthday. No amplifier. I don't need it, yet. It's an acoustic guitar. Wood body, fancy inlays, big hole in the middle. Nylon strings so I don't blister my fingers too much. I've taken a few lessons, and so far, my teacher says I'm catching on really fast. She's got me learning chords, strumming techniques, things like that. I'm going to start taking singing lessons soon, too. My mom says I have a great voice. She listens to country music singers on the radio all the time, and says I sound just as good as any of them. So, I'm going to keep working at it, getting better, and when I'm old enough, I'll head on down to Nashville to make my big break into the music industry. My mom says I can make it. With support like that, how can I go wrong?

DUMPED

Your friends are supposed to be your friends, no matter what. No matter who you are, or who their other friends are. Or what other groups either of you hang out with. There are some bonds that just shouldn't be broken. But when someone you thought was a good friend starts spending less and less time with you, and more and more time with someone else, you have to wonder why. Was it something you said? Something you did? You doubt yourself. You wonder if you're ever going to be able to make friends with anyone else. Then you find out, that person you thought was your friend, dumped you for someone more popular. That's when you realize that maybe your friend wasn't so much your friend after all. And maybe, you just need to be a little more careful about who you decide to hang out with.

BOYFRIEND YET?

"Do you have a boyfriend, yet?" "Do you have a boyfriend, yet?"
They keep saying that to me. Those girls who hang out together are
mean, nasty, and relentless. They go around giggling and teasing
anyone who's not one of them. Just because I'm not in their "cool"
group, they think they have to tease me for not having a boyfriend.
Like I'm not pretty enough, or smart enough, or popular enough.
Yeah, well, when we've all graduated, and I've got the best grades, I
get the best job, and I'm the popular one, I hope I get to see them
still figuring their lives out, so I can walk past them with my
successful husband and say, "Do you have a life, yet?"

FRIEND IN NEED

John's my best bud. He's a smart guy. Planned on going to college,
getting a degree in computer engineering. He and his parents had
everything all worked out. They were setting money aside for his
education so he could pay for all his classes, books, everything he
needed. Then his dad got cancer, had to leave his job, and spent lots
of time in the hospital. The money ran out fast and the debt piled up.
John had to drop out of college, get a job to try and pay the bills. His
dreams of a college degree were over. Me, I had finally saved up ten
thousand dollars for the old red Mustang I'd been wanting to buy for
the last two years. I'd been dreaming about that car. About cruising
around, looking cool, catching everyone's eye. Washing it in the
driveway on Sundays so the neighbors could all see it. Priorities,
right? Well, let's just say, I'm getting around fine without the car,
and my best bud John is back in college.

SURVIVAL

Okay, all this talk of creationism, the big bang, parallel universes, black holes, curved space, it all makes my head spin. I don't really care how we got here, or what lies beyond our solar system. I just want to know what we're going to do about our planet right now. Economy, ecology, global warming, poisoning of our waters, mining of the Earth, destruction of our forests. When I retire, if I'm lucky enough to live that long, what's going to be left? Will my children have a chance for a future? When I'm ready, will I even be able to have children? Please, can we stop arguing about what we'll never know and start talking about what we can do to keep ourselves from extinction? I'm not asking a lot. I just want to survive. I want all of us to survive.

BENNY DIED

Benny died. Benny died. That's all they said to me. My mom and dad gave me no more information about the death of my little brother than they'd give about the weather. It's cold. It's raining. Benny died. How was I supposed to handle that? Did they even think for one moment what that did to me? I mean, it was horrible enough that I'd just lost my little brother, my little punk buddy, without hearing the news delivered in such an emotionless manner. Did they really not care that he died, or how I felt about it? Did they care just as little about me? Why was I even there? How did he die? Was I next? Then I saw it on the news. "Couple throws child off Foresthill Bridge". Maybe I would have been next. It's raining.

PAYBACK

Sometimes you don't know what someone who you thought was your friend is doing to you until it's too late. I had my eye on Lisa for the longest time. She didn't know me very well, but I wanted to ask her out and show her that I was a stand-up guy. That I was someone she could really enjoy spending time with. Who knows? Maybe it could have turned into something serious and we could have spent the rest of our lives together. I shared my feelings about her with my friend Matt. I guess he agreed that she seemed like a great girl, and he decided to approach her for himself. He told her I was a loser, and that she should stay away from me. Some friend, huh? Well, a few months later, I heard she went all wacko and stabbed him in the arm with a pencil before leaving him for someone else. I guess I can stop thinking about how to get back at him for what he did to me. Payback happened all on its own. I'm okay with that.

THE TRUTH

You wanna know the truth? Here's the truth. I never cared about you. I never wanted to be there for you. I never loved you. You were nothing to me. You are nothing to me. And when I saw you with him, that didn't mean anything to me, either. So don't apologize to me, don't try to spare my feelings, and don't try to let me down easy. I don't need that from you. I don't need anything from you. So, just, just, don't. Because, I never really loved you. Not really.

DECISIONS

To college or not to college, that is the question. Whether it's nobler to bite the bullet, put your parents in debt, and study for the next four years, or find a low paying job, work your way up, and hope that four years later you're making what you would have had you gotten a degree in something. Years of paying off student loans, or saving money for a house? Or for retirement? Or work part time and go to a trade school? What do I want to do for the rest of my life? I really don't think it's fair, having to make such big decisions this early in life. If I go to college, I don't know what career will hold opportunities for me by the time I graduate, what will sustain me, or what I'll be happy doing for the next forty years. I'm not prepared to make these kinds of decisions. There's so much room for error. Heck, I don't even know what I want for dinner tonight.

HITTING ENTER

I was mad at my creative writing teacher for giving me a bad critique on my last assignment. He said my prose was weak, my story was cliché and my characters were flat. So just to make myself feel better, I began writing an email to him, telling him that he didn't know what he was talking about. About how his assessment of my work was weak, explaining my characters in greater depth, giving him back story on the protagonist, and explaining why the dialogue was short and written with an Australian accent. I said that if he couldn't understand that, that he shouldn't be a teacher. Of course I never intended to send it. My little brother came in, asked me what I was doing, and accidentally hit send. I figured I was sure to fail the class after that. When I showed up to class the next day, the teacher had printed my email and graded it. He laid it on my desk and walked away. He had given my email a B+, and noted, "Much better. Watch your spelling."

BAD HOLIDAYS

I just wish they'd stop fighting. Holidays suck at my house. That's the time when both my parents have more time off work, which just means they have more time to yell at each other. And nothing is ever right, ever good enough. The tree's not decorated right, the lights aren't strung properly, the turkey's too dry, there's not enough money for presents, whatever. It's always got to be something. If I ever get married and have kids, I don't care what's going on, Christmas is going to be about them. I don't want to ruin it by squabbling about things that just aren't that important. I just want to see the family, together, gathered around the tree or the dining room table, being thankful for what we have. Yeah, that would be good. That would be a good holiday.

CHEMISTRY

She was the most beautiful girl in school. I'd been wanting to talk to her for the longest time, but I couldn't work up the courage. When I saw her in the hall the other day, I finally decided it was time. I walked right up to her and asked her if she wanted to go with me to the park. She said that we had chemistry. I agreed with her. I told her there was something very special between us. Some unseen, deep power that brought us together, and that it was a wonderful thing that we could finally recognize that. Like it was meant to be. Like it was written in the stars. That we really did have a unique chemistry between us. Then she looked in my eyes, and placed a finger on my lips. She leaned forward and said, "Chemistry. We have Chemistry 101 in three minutes. Got your books?"

PRINCESS ME

I'm a princess. Not because I was born into royalty, or married into it, but because I was made to be a princess. My mother dresses me like one, and my father spoils me like one. And everyone who sees me knows I'm a princess. I stand tall, and walk with pride everywhere I go. People stand aside and point at me as I walk, obviously in awe of all that I am. I sometimes hear them say things like, "Wow. Look at her. What a princess." And they laugh and laugh. I understand. They can't help themselves. I'm sure they just laugh because they're nervous about being around such royalty as me. After all, I am a princess.

SLEEP FLYING

Ever since I can remember, I've had dreams about flying. Not in airplanes. I mean, flying all by myself. I would push myself off the ground with a little kick, and move my arms, pushing myself through the air, like I was swimming. But above the trees, not in the water. Sometimes the dreams are so real, I tell myself it's not a dream. That I'm really flying. That this time it finally came true, and I now have the ability to do what I'd only dreamt of doing. Of course, then I wake up and I can't fly. It's such a wonderful thing at the time, flying like that. Maybe I can apply some of that to real life, though. If I have dreams, goals, for my life, and I work hard enough at them, perhaps I can achieve those things, and have other abilities I've only dreamt of. That's one way to fly.

BOOK REPORT

I don't mind doing book reports for school. I enjoy sharing stories, explaining the characters and what motivates them, and how everything works out in the end. It's a good feeling when you present your book report in front of the class, and you can see the other students being genuinely interested in what you're saying. When you can pull them into the story and make them feel like they're part of it. Like they're right there with the characters, hearing what they're saying, seeing what they're seeing, and taking the adventure with them. Yeah, I like doing book reports. I just hate having to go through all the time and trouble of reading the book first.

CAMPGROUND LADIES

All summer long my parents plan for our fall camping trip. Like it's a grand, momentous event. Like we haven't been doing it every year since I was six. Like we don't burn the hot dogs, sleep on lumpy ground, and come home with colds and mosquito bites every time. The only good thing, is that I'm getting older now, and the girls I meet at the campground keep looking better and better to me. Of course, just when I get the courage to introduce myself, the trip is over, and everyone has to go home. Maybe this time I'll make my presence known sooner. Maybe this trip will be a good one. I think I'll start packing my gear early this year.

ROUGH AGE

This is a rough age. More school work, more chores and responsibility at home, more people to meet, and more names to remember. Last year was a rough age. Changing schools, being one of the youngest, learning where the classrooms were, remembering the combination to a new locker, the new teachers, and avoiding new bullies. And reconnecting with the bullies who were one year ahead of me last year, who are in my new school, and still one year ahead of me. In a couple of years, when it's time to move up to the next school, that'll be a rough age, too. I hear my parents talk about how rough it is for them, being their age, with all their responsibilities, jobs, bills, and slowing down, being tired from all of it. I guess any age is a rough age. You just have to make the best of it.

CREATIVE TIME

I'm a writer. I know, I'm young, but I am a writer. Blogs, poems, short novels. Thinking about writing a screenplay. Only thing is, I keep getting distracted. Drama class, sports, homework. Those things are okay, they're good things, and they help me to grow and learn. The bad things are television, Sudoku puzzles, video games, things like that. I keep finding myself being drawn to them. When I write, I can get lost in my writing, and it's a beautiful thing. It's creative, and I'm almost always proud of what I've written. When I spend a lot of time on it, or even write a little at a time over a long period, even I'm amazed at what I can accomplish. Then I think about how much time I've spent working puzzles or playing games, and wonder how much I could have written in that time. I think I'm going to schedule creative time every day, and dedicate it to nothing but writing. Maybe two or three hours a day. I'm pretty sure I'll be happy with the results. And hopefully, so will my readers.

SCENES FOR TEENS

WHO WAS DRIVING?

JACK and CONNIE are standing at the scene of an auto accident. Connie has driven her father's new car over a fire hydrant.

JACK
I don't know what I can do for you, Connie. This is your mess.

CONNIE
I don't want you to do anything. I just want you to be here for me.

Connie snuggles up to Jack. Jack puts his arm around Connie.

JACK
I'm here.

CONNIE
I'm a mess.

JACK
Yeah, you are.

CONNIE
Not helping, Jack.

JACK
Do you want me to call your parents for you?

CONNIE
(perking right up)
Seriously? You'd do that?

JACK
I'd rather not, but I will. If you really need me to.

CONNIE
I do.

JACK
What do you want me to tell them?

CONNIE
That you were driving.

JACK
What?!

CONNIE
Jack--

JACK
Are you nuts!

CONNIE
My parents are gonna kill me!

JACK
My parents would kill me!

CONNIE
Look, you tell my parents you were driving, and I'll tell your parents I was
driving. Then we're both off the hook.

JACK
Do you really think our parents don't talk to each other? And besides, what
do we tell the police and the insurance company?

CONNIE
Leave that to me. Trust me. Now you call my parents, and I'll call yours.
Let's get this over with.

Jack and Connie turn away from each other and dial on their cell phones.

JACK
(reluctantly talking into his cell phone)
Hello, Mr. Anderson? This is Jack Baker. I'm so very sorry, but I was
driving your car, and I ran over a fire hydrant. Yes, Connie's fine. We're
both fine. I'm afraid your car is not.

Jack pulls the phone away from his ear because Mr. Anderson is yelling.

JACK (CONT'D)
Yes, sir. Yes, sir. The police are on their way. Yes, sir.

Jacks hangs up and turns toward Connie. Connie talks into her cell phone,
crying hysterically.

CONNIE

Mr. Baker! Your son Jack was driving my daddy's car and ran over a fire hydrant! My daddy's car is totaled! It's all Jack's fault!

Connie hangs up, then immediately stops crying, turns to Jack, and smiles.

CONNIE
Sorry.

JACK
What?!

Connie looks off and runs away, crying hysterically.

CONNIE
Officer! Officer! Help!

Jack hangs his head in defeat.

END

THE RIGHT PEOPLE

SAMANTHA and JOEY are sitting together in their high school lunch room. Samantha hands Joey some papers.

SAMANTHA
Here you go, Joey.

JOEY
It's done?

SAMANTHA
Yup.

JOEY
Wow, Sam, no one's ever done anything like this for me before.

SAMANTHA
Maybe you're just hanging out with the wrong people.

JOEY
Maybe you're right. Maybe I need to hang out with more people like you.

SAMANTHA
Or, you need to hang out with me more.

JOEY
What?

SAMANTHA
I could be good for you, Joey. We could be good together.

JOEY
Uh, look, Sam, I really wasn't thinking of you in that way.

SAMANTHA
Fine! Do your own homework from now on!

Samantha jumps up and storms away.

JOEY
Hope I get an "A" on this.

END

STARS IN YOUR EYES

JESSICA and CHRISTOPHER are stargazing on a beautiful night.

CHRISTOPHER
Jessica?

JESSICA
Yes, Christopher?

CHRISTOPHER
Have you ever wondered how some things are possible?

JESSICA
Things like what?

CHRISTOPHER
Like, how so much stuff can fit in such small places sometimes?

JESSICA
Not sure I know what you mean.

CHRISTOPHER
I mean, look at all those stars up there. Millions and millions of them.
Filling the entire universe. And yet, they somehow manage to fit all that
into your two, beautiful eyes. And all the joy, humor, and caring in the
world, compacted down and placed in your little heart.

JESSICA
Christopher.

CHRISTOPHER
Yes, Jessica?

JESSICA
I like you, too.

CHRISTOPHER
(smiling big)
Sweet. Sweet.

END

WHAT'S THE POINT?

JILL and BOB are at a funeral, off in a corner of the room.

JILL

I'm so sorry. Is there anything I can do for you?

BOB

You can get me a drink.

JILL

I'd rather not. It's a funeral. You need to keep it together.

BOB

Keep it together? I need to keep it together? What do you think I've been doing for the last two months with Lisa in the hospital?

JILL

I know it's been hard, Bob, but you just need to hang tough for a couple more days. Just until…until the services are over, at least.

BOB

Then what? Can I get drunk then? Huh?

JILL

No, I mean--

BOB

What? What's your point?

JILL

I mean, it's what killed her. Don't let it kill you, too. That's my point.

BOB

Yeah, well maybe that's *my* point.

END

HYPNOTIZED

HAROLD is lying back in a chair, hypnotized. FREDDIE is talking to him.

FREDDIE
You're completely asleep.

HAROLD
I'm completely asleep.

FREDDIE
You are completely under my power.

HAROLD
I am completely under your power.

FREDDIE
When you wake, you will remember none of this conversation.

HAROLD
When I wake, I will remember none of this conversation.

FREDDIE
I'm going to ask you some questions now, Harold. I want you to answer to the best of your ability. Do you understand?

HAROLD
I understand.

FREDDIE
Is your sister Tammy going out with anyone?

HAROLD
No.

FREDDIE
Do you know if Tammy is interested in anyone?

HAROLD
No.

FREDDIE
What are your sister Tammy's favorite flowers?

HAROLD
Pansies.

FREDDIE
What is your sister Tammy's favorite color?

HAROLD
Yellow.

FREDDIE
When you see Tammy, you must tell her that Freddie is a great guy, and
that she should go out with him.

HAROLD
When I see Tammy, I must tell her that Freddie is a yellow pansy.

(Harold opens his eyes and sits up)

HAROLD (CONT'D)
Seriously, Freddie, if you like my sister just tell her.

FREDDIE
What the--

HAROLD
Did you really think you could hypnotize me?

FREDDIE
I, I--

HAROLD
Relax.
(as if in trance)
I will remember none of this conversation.

FREDDIE
Oh, geez.

Harold exits, laughing his head off.

END

IT WASN'T ME

BEN and LAURA meet up after school.

BEN

Laura, who was that I saw you with at the party store this afternoon?

LAURA

What are you talking about? I wasn't at the party store today.

BEN

Sure you were. You were wearing the same outfit even. I know it was you.
Who was that guy?

LAURA

Listen, I said it wasn't me, so it wasn't me. If you're just looking to start an
argument with me, forget it. I'm not biting.

BEN

Okay. You want to play it that way? I'll ask him myself. I've seen him
around the school. Next time I see him, I'll introduce myself. "Hi, I'm Ben.
I'm Laura's boyfriend. Good to meet you."

LAURA

Ben, don't.

BEN

Oh, something to hide?

LAURA

Yes. He's a cop. Undercover. He wanted me to help get evidence against
you for selling drugs.

BEN

That's ridiculous. I don't sell drugs. There is no evidence.

LAURA

Yeah, well, there will be now. Bye, Ben.

END

ABOUT BILL

ANGELA and CARRIE are standing outside their high school, looking at classmate BILL from afar.

ANGELA
What can you tell me about Bill?

CARRIE
What do you mean?

ANGELA
I mean, is he a nice guy, a jerk, a nerd, a jock, what?

CARRIE
Why?

ANGELA
Because he's hot! Duh.

CARRIE
So, why ask me? Why not talk to him and find out for yourself?

ANGELA
I don't want to waste my time talking to him if he's a jerk. I've got better things to do than talk to some guy who doesn't meet my expectations.

CARRIE
You know, Angela, I think you two have a lot in common. You should go for it. You could have a full life together.

ANGELA
Thanks, Carrie! I'm there!

Angela walks quickly away to talk to Bill.

CARRIE
A very full life, seeing as how you're both so full of yourselves.
(calling out to Angela)
Have fun, you two!

END

PRESTIGE

TAYLOR and RILEY are quibbling over who knows more famous people.

TAYLOR
You know, I once ran into Drew Barrymore at the theatre.

RILEY
I heard it was a book signing, and you paid for a ticket to get her
autograph.

TAYLOR
Which reminds me, I once got Drew Barrymore's autograph.

RILEY
Well, I once saw Katy Perry in person.

TAYLOR
It was a concert. I saw her, too. We went there together, remember? We
were in the nosebleed seats. But I was in a movie with Hugh Jackman.

RILEY
You were an extra. So was I. There were nine hundred other extras there.
You didn't even get near him. But I once had lunch with Emma Watson.

TAYLOR
That wasn't *the* Emma Watson from the Harry Potter movies. That was
Emma Jean Watson, the school lunch lady. I was there. But you know who
I got to shake hands with at the Justin Bieber concert? Justin Bieber.

RILEY
You bragging about that?

TAYLOR
Um, no. Never mind.

RILEY
I saw Katy Perry once, in person.

TAYLOR
Hey! Me, too!

RILEY
Now, that's cool.
END

THAT ONE THING
BOBBY and JANET are in the park, sitting on a park bench.

JANET
Bobby? I'm looking forward to the dance this Friday.

BOBBY
Um, Janet, I, uh, I'm not going.

JANET
Not going? What happened? You said you were looking forward to it. That you wanted to dance with me in front of everyone in the school.

BOBBY
That was then.

JANET
Then? That was then? What's happened since then?

BOBBY
Stuff happens. Things change.

JANET
Like what? It was just last week!

BOBBY
Janet, I don't think we have that much in common.

JANET
In common? Both of us are on the swim team, we're both Capricorns, we listen to the same music, we like the same toppings on our pizza. What else is there?

BOBBY
There's that one thing. You know. That one thing you said you'd never do.

JANET
Oh, you have got to be kidding me! I thought you loved me.

BOBBY
Janet, I never said I loved you.

JANET

You said you loved being with me, that you loved the things we do together. That's the same thing.

BOBBY

No, it's not. Look, I enjoy your company. And yes, we do have a few things in common, but you won't do that one thing I want you to do.

JANET

If you cared for me at all, you'd understand that I'm not ready, and you'd respect that.

BOBBY

Not ready? You said never. You said the whole idea was repulsive to you. How am I supposed to continue a serious relationship with someone like that? I have needs!

JANET

Well so do I, Bobby, and one of those is self-respect. How could I look at myself in the mirror if I gave in and did that with you? With anybody?

BOBBY

I'm done with this, Janet. It's over. Donna said she'll do it with me, and she's good at it.

JANET

Donna? Are you kidding me? What level is she even at? What am I saying? I don't even know what the levels are.
(beat)
Fine. If that's what you really want, have fun with Donna and your little Candy Crush Saga. I will never play that dumb game. Never!

Janet rushes off, and Bobby starts playing Candy Crush Saga on his cell phone.

BOBBY

Crush, crush, crush.

END

LOST FEELINGS

TED and MOLLY are sitting on a park bench arguing.

TED

Molly, do you think you could take some time to think this over?

MOLLY

I don't know, Ted. I don't think it's gonna make any difference.

TED

But, why? How do you know that?

MOLLY

Because, what I feel is what I feel.

TED

But, how do you know what you feel until you take time to think about it?

MOLLY

I just know. That's why they're called feelings. You feel them. And I'm just
not feeling this. Not now.

TED

When? When did you feel it? What changed?

MOLLY

It doesn't matter, I'm just not feeling it now, and I'm not going to. And,
nothing changed. I mean, I don't know what changed. It just did.

TED

So you're done with me? That's it? Thanks for everything? I'm moving on?
Good luck, Ted?

Molly pauses for a moment, then leans forward and kisses Ted on the
forehead.

MOLLY

Good luck, Ted.

Molly walks away.

END

AFTER SCHOOL LESSON

JEFF and MIKE are in the lunchroom at school.

JEFF

Kurt said he wants to fight me after school today. What do I do?

MIKE

Do you want to fight him?

JEFF

No!

MIKE

Then don't.

JEFF

Then everyone will think I'm chicken.

MIKE

Then fight him.

JEFF

He'll tear me up. I can't win a fight against him. He's huge.

MIKE

Man, make up your mind. Look, you know if you fight Kurt, you'll lose. You know some people will say you're chicken if you don't fight him. You have to decide what's more important to you, getting your butt kicked to satisfy some jerks who don't have your best interests in mind, or being smart and walking away from this with all your teeth.

JEFF

What would you do?

MIKE

Dude, seriously? Go home. Walk away from Kurt and his idiot friends, and all those jerks who want to see you get pummeled. Why does he want to fight you, anyway? What did you do to tick him off?

JEFF

Nothing. He does this every week. He randomly picks someone he hasn't beat up yet, and schedules a fight by the baseball diamond. It just happened to be me this time. It's like a regular after school event.

MIKE

Okay, do you know any of the other guys Kurt's beaten up recently?

JEFF

Yeah, I know a few of them.

MIKE

There you go. Keep your appointment with Kurt. But before you go, rally up all the guys he's beat up in the past. All of you show up together.

JEFF

Gang up on him?

MIKE

Yes! He beats up on people who are weaker than he is, so, be a strong group and beat up on him. See how he likes it.

JEFF

What if he picks a fight with me next week?

MIKE

Teach him this lesson today, and he'll get the message. You won't have any more trouble with him. I guarantee it.

JEFF

You gonna be there?

MIKE

Nope. I've done my part. I'm going home to spend some quality time with my dinner table. Happy hunting.

END

PROM NIGHT

YVONNE and TIFFANY are in the ladies room, putting on make-up and talking.

YVONNE
Tim said he refuses go to the prom with me.

TIFFANY
Did he say why?

YVONNE
Something about all the sheep dressing silly and lining up for a ridiculous and meaningless social event.

TIFFANY
Really?

YVONNE
Yeah. Apparently he's on this rebellious kick. Thinks if we attend the prom that we're just bowing down and caving in to the system.

TIFFANY
Well, I hope that's not really how he feels. I'd like to think that he realizes this is the last chance he has to do this, and that this'll be something he's going to remember for the rest of his life.

YVONNE
Yeah, you see? That's what I'm talking about.

TIFFANY
That's what I told him.

YVONNE
You told him that?

TIFFANY
Yup. That's why he's going to the prom with me.

END

LEAN ON ME

NATE and RANDY are sitting on the school steps.

NATE

Do you think I could stay at your house tonight, Randy?

RANDY

Yeah, I think so. Of course I'd have to check with my folks, but I don't think they'd mind. Why? What's up?

NATE

My parents have been getting into it lately. I need a break. I just can't listen to them fighting every single night.

RANDY

Man, that's not cool. Yeah, man, maybe my folks will let you stay a few nights.

NATE

Thanks, but I'll take this one night at a time. I kind of want to keep watch that it doesn't get too out of hand, you know.

RANDY

So, Nate, like, what are they fighting about?

NATE

Anything and everything. I think they just don't want to be together anymore, and they don't know how to end it. Neither one wants to be the one to leave, so they just keep fighting. Maybe that's how they want to live. I don't know.

RANDY

That's sad. But, hey, for now, you can lean on me, bro.

NATE

Thanks, bro.

END

POOR BOOTSIE

DAVE and SANDY are standing under a willow tree.

DAVE
I'm so depressed, Sandy. I really can't be alone right now.

SANDY
Oh, what's wrong, Dave?

DAVE
My dog, Bootsie. He...he's gone.

SANDY
Oh, no. I'm so sorry to hear that. What happened?

DAVE
Poor Bootsie. He chased a squirrel out into the street, and, and, I can't bear
it. Could you hold me, please?

Sandy puts her arms around Dave and rocks him back and forth.

SANDY
Oh, you poor thing. I can't imagine how you must feel.

DAVE
Yeah, poor Bootsie. He went doing what he loved most. Chasing squirrels.
He was the greatest dog ever.

SANDY
I know. You always told me Bootsie was your best friend.

Dave puts his arms around Sandy and squeezes tight.

SANDY (CONT'D)
Wait, Bootsie with the white paws? I thought he was your cat.

DAVE
Yeah, and he's fine. But I got my hug!

Sandy slaps Dave and storms off. Dave rubs his face and smiles.

END

BIG BROTHER

SAM is watching TV. His younger sister BARBARA enters and sees that Sam has a black eye.

                    BARBARA
          Wow, what happened to you, Sam?

                    SAM
          Nothing.

                    BARBARA
          Nothing? You got a black eye.

                    SAM
          I don't wanna talk about it, Barbara.

                    BARBARA
     Well, I do. Nobody hits my big brother and gets away with it.

                    SAM
          It's okay. I didn't get the worst of it.

                    BARBARA
          Hm. Then, good for you, I guess.

                    SAM
          Mom got pizza for dinner.

                    BARBARA
     Sounds good. Don't change the subject. What happened?

                    SAM
          Leave it alone, will you?

                    BARBARA
     Don't bite my head off. I'm just concerned about you, that's all.

                    SAM
          Burt Carson.

                    BARBARA
               (pausing)
     What about Burt Carson? How do you know him?

SAM
He's the one with two black eyes.

BARBARA
He started a fight with you?

SAM
Not so much. Well, indirectly, yeah, I guess he did.

BARBARA
I know Burt Carson.

SAM
I know you do.

BARBARA
He's been saying bad things about me.

SAM
I know.

BARBARA
They're all lies.

SAM
He won't be saying them again.

Barbara takes a moment to let it all sink in. She smiles at Sam.

BARBARA
I love you, big brother.

SAM
Pizza's in the kitchen.

Barbara gives Sam a hug and exits.

END

APOLOGY

MELISSA is leaning against a tree. JACKIE walks up.

JACKIE
Melissa, can we talk?

MELISSA
Sure, I guess. What about?

JACKIE
Look, when I first told Eddie I'd go out with him, I had no idea you two
were dating.

MELISSA
Oh, okay. You didn't see us sitting together at lunch, you didn't see us
hanging out after school, and you didn't see us walking together at the
mall. Got it.

JACKIE
Melissa, I thought you two were just friends. That's what Eddie told me.

MELISSA
Then Eddie lied to you, just like he did to me. Anyway, Jackie, he's your
problem now.

JACKIE
Not exactly. I saw him at the mall with Angie. I think he's her problem
now.

MELISSA
So, you're not seeing each other anymore?

JACKIE
No. That's why I wanted to talk to you. I just wanted to apologize.

MELISSA
Eh, I'm over it. And him.

JACKIE
Well, either way, I'm sorry.

END

BABYSITTING NIGHTMARE

AMANDA and JAMIE are sitting on the floor at Amanda's house.

AMANDA

Oh, my, goodness! Those kids were monsters! If I had known what wild brats they were going to be, I never would have agreed to be their babysitter.

JAMIE

They're two year old twin girls. How horrible could they be?

AMANDA

Ever hear the term, "Terrible twos?" There's a reason they say that. They're possessed!

JAMIE

I don't get it. You feed them, you put them to bed, you watch television until the parents get home. How hard is that?

AMANDA

No, you don't get it. Yeah, they're cute, at first. The smiles, reaching out to hug you...then the parents leave and all heck breaks loose.

JAMIE

Ha, ha! Seriously.

AMANDA

Don't you laugh! Don't think for one minute you have any clue what these kids are like. The cartoons, the cookies, the screaming and crying...all night long!

JAMIE

So, I take it you quit?

AMANDA

You kidding? No! It pays ten bucks an hour. I'm going back tonight.

END

NEW DRESS

SUE is modeling her new dress for her boyfriend CHUCK.

SUE
Why do you have to be so mean?

CHUCK
I'm not being mean. I'm being truthful. Don't you want me to tell you the truth?

SUE
Of course I do, but I still think there's a more tactful way you could have said that.

CHUCK
I'm sorry, honey, but that really is the ugliest dress I've ever seen.

SUE
Then stop looking at it!

CHUCK
I'm not looking at the dress. I'm looking at you, and how beautiful you are, despite the dress.

SUE
Really?

CHUCK
Really.

SUE
You think I'm beautiful?

CHUCK
Of course I do. Your face, your hair, your eyes, your sweet smile, your shining personality...

SUE
Chuck.

CHUCK
Yes, Sue.

SUE
Laying it on a bit thick there, don't you think?

CHUCK
Really?

SUE
Really.

CHUCK
Just telling you how I feel.

SUE
You think you're getting out of this that easy?

CHUCK
Love you.

SUE
Love you. I'll go get the matching shoes.

Sue exits. Chuck mumbles to himself.

CHUCK
That dress has got to go.

SUE (O.C.)
I heard that!

END

PAWN SHOP

HAILEY and KEVIN are in a pawn shop.

KEVIN
Hailey, this is my only guitar amp.

HAILEY
Kevin, you know we have priorities. We already had this discussion.

KEVIN
I know, but--

HAILEY
Eh, eh, eh. Priorities. The man said we could get two hundred dollars for that amp.

KEVIN
I know, but--

HAILEY
Eh, eh, eh. That money can be used for much more important things.

KEVIN
But what do I play my guitar through when I'm practicing with the band?

HAILEY
Plug into the bass player's amp. It'll sound just fine.

KEVIN
If you say so. I'm sure you know what's best.

HAILEY
I do. Speaking of, "I, do"...
(talking to a pawn shop employee)
Yes, I was told we could get two hundred dollars for this guitar amp. We'd like to put it down on an engagement ring you have in your showcase.

Kevin screams, grabs the guitar amp, and runs out the door.

HAILEY (CONT'D)
Kevin! Get back here!

END

GOING AWAY

SHERRIE and WILL are sitting on a front porch swing.

SHERRIE
Will, I don't know what to say.

WILL
You've said it, Sherrie. You're going away to State. I'm stuck here at Community College and you're leaving.

SHERRIE
I have to, Will. I got accepted. If I don't go, my parents won't pay for me to go to college here.

WILL
So I'm stuck here while you go make a real career for yourself.

SHERRIE
What am I supposed to do, huh? Pass up college? Pass on a career? Hope that you'll support me?

WILL
Oh, I can't possibly support you where I'm going, right?

SHERRIE
I didn't say that.

WILL
Then stay. We'll get jobs and work our way through school here.

SHERRIE
Will, you know I can't do that. I can't pass up this opportunity.

WILL
But you can pass on us?

SHERRIE
No. I mean...I...why do you have to do this?

WILL
Why do you have to act like you're so much better than me?

SHERRIE

Better? Why, because I worked to get good grades and I got accepted and you didn't?

WILL

See, there you go! That's what I'm talking about.

SHERRIE

Will, I have a chance to do something good for myself here. Why can't you just be happy for me?

WILL

Because I'm not going with you!

SHERRIE
(beat)
I'm not going away forever.

WILL

Are you sure?

SHERRIE

Pretty sure. I'm gonna get my degree, and I'm gonna come back here, get a good job, and we can live our lives together just like we planned. But more financially secure.

WILL

I guess I'll stick it out here.

SHERRIE

You'll wait for me?

WILL

Of course. I love you.

SHERRIE
I know.

END

MAGIC POWERS

DARLENE and ERIC, two strangers in a video store, are having a tug of war with a DVD of the latest Harry Potter movie.

DARLENE
You know my powers are stronger than yours, right?

ERIC
I seriously doubt that, but if it makes you feel better, I won't argue with you about it.

DARLENE
It sounds to me like you're doing just that.

ERIC
You'd like that, wouldn't you? I'm guessing that arguing is one of your greatest powers?

DARLENE
My greatest power is winning.

ERIC
Oh, so sorry. Didn't see that.

DARLENE
My magic is not to be trifled with, good sir. I have powers beyond what you may have ever seen.

ERIC
Ah, but you don't know what I've seen. And I will say, dear lady, I have seen plenty.

DARLENE
Well, obviously you haven't seen the latest Harry Potter movie, or you wouldn't be trying to take it from me.

ERIC
I'm not trying to take it from you. I saw it first.

DARLENE
No, sir. I saw it first.

ERIC
But my hand was on it first.

DARLENE
The gentlemanly thing to do would be to concede to the lady.

Eric thinks for a moment.

ERIC
Perhaps there's another copy on the shelf.

DARLENE
Then let me have this one, and you can have the one on the shelf.

ERIC
I may have a better idea.

DARLENE
Let's hear it.

ERIC
Let's call it a tie. Perhaps if we joined forces and watched this movie together...

DARLENE
...combined our powers...

ERIC
...took the journey simultaneously...

Darlene leans forward and looks deep into Eric's eyes.

DARLENE
...and found the true magic?

ERIC
A union! Of course!

DARLENE
You get the popcorn, I'll pay for the movie.

ERIC
You got it!

Eric lets go of the DVD and Darlene runs off with it.

DARLENE
Sorceress exitus!

ERIC
Argh! Foiled again!

END

NEW TATTOO

SUSAN and JANET are sitting on the curb outside Susan's house.

SUSAN
I'm afraid to go in the house.

JANET
Why? What's going on?

SUSAN
My parents told me if I ever got a tattoo, they'd ground me until I was thirty.

JANET
What? You got a tattoo? Are you out of your mind?

SUSAN
Yeah. I don't know what I was thinking.

JANET
That's insane. Maybe you can hide it from them.

SUSAN
No way. My parents have a way of knowing everything.

JANET
Well, it was nice knowing you. Susan.

SUSAN
Thanks a lot. You're not helping.

JANET
What do you want me to say, that was brilliant?

SUSAN
You're my friend. You could be a little more supportive.

JANET
I'm sorry. You're right. What's it a tattoo of?

SUSAN
This is embarrassing.

JANET
Out with it.

SUSAN
Okay. Fine. It's a unicorn jumping over a rainbow.

JANET
(laughing hysterically)
A unicorn jumping over a rainbow? Ha! You're kidding! That's precious!
You *are* insane!

SUSAN
Still not helping, Janet.

JANET
I can't help it. I can't believe you did that. Okay, let me see it.

SUSAN
You don't want to see it.

JANET
Sure I do.

SUSAN
Okay. But no more laughing.

JANET
I'll do my best. Where is it?

SUSAN
Right here.

Susan pulls a paper rub-on tattoo from her pocket and hands it to Janet.

JANET
Seriously? You *should* be grounded until you're thirty!

Janet throws the paper tattoo over her shoulder and walks away. Susan
busts out laughing.

END

BEST MAN

WALT and ANGIE are standing under a tree at the park.

ANGIE

Walt, your brother asked you to be the best man at his wedding. That's a really big deal. You should be happy for him.

WALT

I am, Angie. Really. He's got a great girl, a good job, and they're looking to buy a house. I think their future looks bright.

ANGIE

So, why are you looking depressed?

WALT

I'm not depressed. I was just thinking.

ANGIE

What about?

WALT

Well, he did well in school, got a scholarship, graduated, landed a nice position in a big company, and got the girl of his dreams.

ANGIE

Those are all good things, right?

WALT

Yeah, but I'm, I'm, a little jealous.

ANGIE

Why? He's older than you. You still have time to do those things.

WALT

My grades could be better. And I'm hoping I'll be good enough to get the girl of my dreams.

ANGIE

Who's that?

WALT

(pausing)

You, Angie.

ANGIE
Really? Me?

WALT
Yes. And I know I need to study more and work on a plan for college. But if I can, if I can do well, would you, do you think...

ANGIE
Do I think you can accomplish those things?

WALT
Yeah.

ANGIE
Yes. I have confidence in you. I know you can do anything you put your mind to.

WALT
Do you think I could win the girl of my dreams?

ANGIE
(smiling)
I think it's a strong possibility. And, Walt?

WALT
Yes.

ANGIE
When the time comes, maybe you can ask your brother to be your best man.

WALT
I'd like that.

ANGIE
I think your future looks bright.

WALT
Me, too.

They walk away, holding hands.

END

ROAD TRIP

CHRIS and PAT are sitting on Pat's porch.

CHRIS
I'm bored.

PAT
So, let's get unbored.

CHRIS
How?

PAT
Road trip.

CHRIS
Road trip? Where?

PAT
Where have you always wanted to go, but never went?

CHRIS
The moon.

PAT
Duh. In a car. Where would you like to drive to that you've never been?

CHRIS
I don't know. Disney World, Disneyland.

PAT
What are you, like, ten?

CHRIS
Hey, I never got to go when I was a kid.

PAT
Poor you. Okay, how about someplace that's less than a day's drive?

CHRIS
How about that new mall in Springfield? I hear they've got an arcade there
that puts the one at the mall here to shame.

PAT
Sounds good to me.

CHRIS
Sweet. Who's driving?

PAT
You are. My dad won't let me use the car after I spilled my chocolate shake the last time I drove it. He's still trying to scrub that stuff off the seats and out of the CD player.

CHRIS
My dad won't let me drive since last week when I drove over that stop sign. You'd think they'd make those things easier to see.

PAT
Maybe we can get your mom to take us.

CHRIS
Lame. And she wouldn't drive us three hours just to go to an arcade, anyway.

PAT
Hey, arcade! We've got an arcade at the mall here. Wanna walk there?

CHRIS
Yeah! Road trip!

PAT
Road trip!

END

SUNBURN

JADE and WILLOW are in the gym locker room at school. Jade is in pain.

WILLOW
Jade, what happened to you?

JADE
Sssssssssunburn! It hurts!

WILLOW
Wow. You're like, a toasted tomato. What happened?

JADE
I took my little brother, Charlie, to the beach yesterday. He wanted to go swimming, and my parents were busy, so they had me take the little brat. I decided to make the best of it and get a tan while I was there.

WILLOW
That's not a tan, that's a coat of lobster red.

JADE
I don't get it. I put suntan oil on. Lots of it.

WILLOW
What level of sunblock did you use?

JADE
I don't know, Willow. Charlie gave it to me. Said he didn't want his favorite big sister to burn.

WILLOW
Still got the bottle?

JADE
Yeah. Here it is.

Jade pulls a bottle from her bag and hands it to Willow.

WILLOW
Jade, this is baby oil.

JADE
Charlie!!!
END

WOOD SHOP
COOPER and FINN are talking in woodworking class at school.

COOPER
Finn, did you finish your shop project for your final grade?

FINN
Yeah. I decided to make something on the lathe. I love woodturning.

COOPER
Sweet. What did you make?

FINN
Well, I started out making a huge wood vase. But that didn't go so well.

COOPER
Why not?

FINN
I guess I didn't use the carving tools right. It kept chunking the wood away. So I decided to make a baseball bat instead.

COOPER
Nice. Gonna use it in the game tomorrow?

FINN
No. I cut it too deep, so I decided to make a pool cue out of it.

COOPER
And how did that turn out?

FINN
Not so good. I ended up whittling it down to a toothpick. Here it is. What do you think? Nice?

COOPER
Finn, you got that from the cafeteria. You didn't do your project, did you?

FINN
Nope. Think I'll get a passing grade?

COOPER
Nope.
END

VIGILANTE

HUDSON and MAX are in the schoolyard having a serious conversation.

HUDSON
Max, it isn't worth it, man. You gotta let it go.

MAX
Would you? Would you let it go? Huh?

HUDSON
Yeah. You could get kicked out of school for this.

MAX
It would be worth it to loosen a few of Justin's pretty little teeth.

HUDSON
No, it wouldn't. He's the jerk, but if you hit him, you get kicked out of
school, or worse. You could get prosecuted. Justin would heal. Your record
wouldn't.

MAX
Then what am I supposed to do, Hudson? He took Holly from me. We
were doing great as a couple until he came along, smiling, all smooth
talking, hitting on her. Now they're the great couple.

HUDSON
Pull it in, Max. This wasn't all Justin's doing. I hate to break it to you,
man, but as easy as it was for Justin to talk Holly into breaking up with you
and going out with him, I've got to think that either she wasn't that into
you in the first place, or she's so fickle, she's gonna leave him soon and go
out with the next guy that sweet talks her.

MAX
You think so? Maybe I should sweet talk her and get her back. You think?

HUDSON
I think you need to go home, Max. Forget about her, and just go home.

END

CLOWN MAKEUP
JUDY walks in on ADELLE, who is applying makeup, and screams.

JUDY
Aaaahhhh! Adelle! What happened to you? Your face! You look like you got run over by a beauty supply truck!

ADELLE
Thanks! You like it?

JUDY
Um, I mean, don't you think you overdid it a little?

ADELLE
I don't think so. You need all this stuff. I read up on how to apply everything. A light base to cover the freckles, rouge to heighten the cheekbones, eyeliner to accentuate the eyes, and eye shadow to give depth and color. I followed the directions very carefully.

JUDY
Where did you read that?

ADELLE
Cosmo. Does it look good?

JUDY
Did the instructions say anything about using a mirror?

ADELLE
I didn't think about that.

Adelle turns and looks in the mirror, and screams.

ADELLE (CONT'D)
Aaaahhhh! Quick! Judy! Help! Hand me the makeup remover!

JUDY
Here you go, Bozo.

Judy hands Adelle the makeup remover. Adelle frantically removes the makeup as Judy walks out, laughing.

END

LETTING HER GO

KYLE and WALTER are at Walter's girlfriend's funeral.

WALTER
I let her go.

KYLE
You had to, eventually, man. You gotta move on with your life.

WALTER
No, I don't think you understand.

KYLE
Sure I do. You have to get past the past and focus on your future.

WALTER
I had her. I had her.

KYLE
And now you don't. It could happen to anyone.

WALTER
I had hold of her hand. She was in the water. I was in the canoe. I knew she couldn't swim. She was sinking. I let her go.

KYLE
Man, you couldn't hold on forever. You gotta quit blaming yourself. You had to give out at some point.

WALTER
I didn't give out. I just, decided, to let her go. And I did.

KYLE
Oh.
(beat)
Oh!

END

MISSING

DREW and LOGAN are in a treehouse having a serious heart-to-heart talk.

DREW

Logan, you can't stay in my little brother's treehouse forever. You're going to have to go home sometime. Everybody's looking for you.

LOGAN

I don't have to go home, Drew. I'm not going home. Ever.

DREW

And what am I supposed to say when people start asking questions?

LOGAN

Lie.

DREW

I'm not going to do that. Everyone's worried about you. Your mother's been all over the neighborhood looking for you. She's already called the police. She thinks you may have been kidnapped or something.

LOGAN

She doesn't care where I am. And she knows I left on my own after our last fight.

DREW

Fight over what? What was so bad that you'd want to put her through this?

LOGAN

About my little sister. My mother babies her and ignores me.

DREW

Maybe because your sister needs her help, and you don't. You can take care of yourself, and your mother knows that. That doesn't mean she doesn't love you. All you're doing now is causing her to worry. You're hurting her. Do you really want to do that?

LOGAN

It's like she spends all her time with my sister. Like I don't even exist. I just wish she would spend more time with me like she used to.

DREW

You miss that?

LOGAN
Yeah. I do.

DREW
So tell her that. It's the only way she'll know.

LOGAN
It doesn't matter. I really don't care anyway. I was just blowing off steam.

Logan thinks for a moment, then gets up to leave.

DREW
Where you going?

LOGAN
I'll see you at school tomorrow. I'm going home.

END

MONEY TROUBLES

EMERSON and PAUL are sitting in Paul's garage.

EMERSON

Paul, dude, buddy, can I borrow ten bucks?

PAUL

Seriously? You just borrowed ten bucks from me yesterday. And five the day before that. Then there was last week. I think you owe me like, fifty bucks or something.

EMERSON

No way, man. It's like, thirty-five. I've been keeping track. I want to make sure I pay you back in full. I got it all written in a ledger at home.

PAUL

Then I think you forgot to write a couple of transactions down.

EMERSON

No, I got you covered, bro. So, listen, can I borrow fifteen bucks?

PAUL

Fifteen? I thought you said you wanted ten.

EMERSON

Yeah, ten would be great. Thanks, man.

PAUL

But...you...you just...you. Emerson, what do you need it for?

EMERSON

If I told you it wouldn't be a surprise.

PAUL

Surprise?

EMERSON

Yeah, man. You don't want to spoil the surprise, do you?

PAUL

What surprise?

EMERSON

The big purchase I've been saving up for. For your surprise birthday gift...I mean...oh, man. You just ruined it.

PAUL

My birthday's not for another six months.

EMERSON

Great. I've still got plenty of time to plan.

PAUL

Really, what do you need the money for?

EMERSON

Tacos, dude. I'm hungry.

PAUL

Doesn't your mother feed you?

EMERSON

Yeah, but that's like, not for another hour.

PAUL

Go home, Emerson.

END

TRAFFIC VIOLATIONS

THEO and DAVIS are standing outside the courthouse.

THEO

Davis, aren't you getting tired of this, yet? Having to come to court to pay money and answer for all these tickets?

DAVIS

Yeah, but what can I do? They keep targeting me. Picking on me. It's like they're watching my every move. Just waiting for me to trip up so they can slap me with another ticket. I think that's how they keep paying for all those doughnuts.

THEO

There's no need to be disrespectful. The cops didn't break the law. You did.

DAVIS

Theo, really? You're taking their side on this?

THEO

Let's see. You've been ticketed for speeding twice, running a stop sign, turning without signaling three times, and you've racked up fourteen parking tickets. Whose fault do you think that is?

DAVIS

I was only going in the store for five minutes. It wasn't worth putting money in the meter for.

THEO

Hey, Davis. You want to know how to get out of paying for all these tickets?

DAVIS

Yeah! Tell me! How?

THEO

Stop breaking the law.

DAVIS

Thanks, Officer Theo.

END

HAIR DYE DISASTER

JULIA and NANCY are in Julia's bedroom. Julia is crying. Her hair is five different colors.

JULIA
Oh, my, goodness! What am I going to do? This is a mess!

NANCY
Don't worry, Julia, we'll figure something out.

JULIA
You said that four colors ago, Nancy.

NANCY
I know, but there's got to be something else we can try.

JULIA
I think we've gone through every product Clairol carries.

NANCY
Maybe we should read the instructions this time.

JULIA
It's useless. I'm never going out in public again. My life is over.

NANCY
Look, it could be worse. You hair could fall out.

JULIA
My hair's gonna fall out?

NANCY
No, that's not what I said. Listen, I think I have an idea.

Nancy leaves, and comes back with a wig.

JULIA
A rainbow clown wig? Are you kidding me?

NANCY
Yeah, you're right. Doesn't look much different.

Julia runs away crying.
END

NOT YOUR DECISION

ASHLEY and RYAN are standing on Ryan's front porch.

ASHLEY
I'm not going. I don't care what they say.

RYAN
Ashley, they're your parents, your family. You have to go with them.

ASHLEY
Maybe I could stay here with you. Your parents could be my legal
guardians.

RYAN
You know that's not gonna happen.

ASHLEY
Why, Ryan? Don't you want me to stay? Don't you love me?

RYAN
Of course I want you to stay. Of course I love you. But this is out of our
control.

ASHLEY
So, my whole family gets uprooted because my dad got a job in Phoenix,
and I'll never see you again. What am I supposed to do, just live with it?
Not try to find a solution?

RYAN
Look, I'm not happy about it, either, but sometimes we have to live with
what's handed to us.

ASHLEY
I'll run away. I'll stay with friends. I'll move around. I'm not leaving here.
I'm not leaving you. I've decided. That's it.

RYAN
Ashely, I wish it could be that way, but it's not your decision to make. You
have to be with your family. It'll work out in the end. If we're meant to be,
we'll find a way back to each other. Really. Trust me.

END

FIVE DOLLAR SPECIAL

ANDREW and NOAH are in a booth at a restaurant. Andrew has the bill.

ANDREW

Okay, Noah. Let's see. You had fries, a cheeseburger, and three waters. That's four bucks for the fries, eight fifty for the burger, and two bucks each for the waters. That's eighteen fifty plus a four buck tip. Give me twenty-two fifty for your part and I'll go up and pay the bill.

NOAH

What? Twenty-two fifty? No way!

ANDREW

Okay, cheapskate. Just give me twenty even and I'll take care of your half of the tip.

NOAH

Andrew, the cheeseburger meal was a five dollar special, and the water is free.

ANDREW

Didn't you get tomatoes and onions on your burger? Ice and straws with your water?

NOAH
Yeah.

ANDREW

That stuff's extra, man. It adds up.

Noah snatches the bill from Andrew's hands and looks at it.

NOAH

Hey, the whole bill's only ten bucks. What's your deal?

ANDREW

I, uh, don't have any money. Can you spot me a few bucks for the food?

NOAH

I have a better idea. (yelling to the waitress) Excuse me! My friend wants to wash dishes for you!

END

NO EVIDENCE
APRIL and SANDY are looking over some stolen goods at Sandy's house.

APRIL
You're not gonna get away with this, Sandy.

SANDY
Sure I am. Unless you squeal on me. You gonna squeal on me, April?
Huh?

APRIL
No.

SANDY
Then why am I not gonna get away with it?

APRIL
The police have ways of figuring these things out.

SANDY
There's no evidence, April. I was careful. I thought it all through.

APRIL
How do you know you didn't miss anything? What about fingerprints?

SANDY
I wore gloves.

APRIL
Credit card for the little you *did* pay for?

SANDY
I paid cash.

APRIL
Security cameras?

SANDY
(beat) Oh...no. Oh...no.

END

BAD FALL

JANE is on campus grounds, leaning against a tree, in an angry mood. ELLA, seeming troubled, approaches.

ELLA
Jane, did you hear about Bobby?

JANE
Hear what? He's being a jerk again?

ELLA
No. Jane, listen--

JANE
I know, he's going out with Tracy.

ELLA
Jane, this is serious.

JANE
More serious than Bobby cheating on me?

ELLA
Tracy said they just took him to the hospital in an ambulance.

JANE
Oh, no. What happened?

ELLA
Tracy said Bobby was running down the stairs and tripped. He had a real bad fall. Hit his head and got knocked out.

JANE
What hospital did they take him to?

ELLA
I don't know. I'm guessing St. John's. It's the closest. You wanna go there and see if he's all right?

JANE
I'll drive.

END

FIDELITY

GABE and AUSTIN are sitting on the grass at school during lunch.

AUSTIN
Gabe, check her out. Over there by the tree.

GABE
Debbie? What about her?

AUSTIN
She's hot. Don't you think she's hot?

GABE
Austin, yeah, she is, but--

AUSTIN
Look at the blonde standing by the door. She's a cutie.

GABE
Okay, I see a nice one.

AUSTIN
Where?

GABE
The brunette sitting at the picnic table over there.

AUSTIN
Dude. Not cool. That's my girlfriend.

GABE
Right. Not cool. You've got a great girl, and you're sitting here scoping out all the other ones.

AUSTIN
A guy's allowed to look.

GABE
And a girl's allow some respect. Go sit with her and show her you appreciate her before some other guy eyes her, shows her the respect she deserves, and takes her from you.

Austin pauses, then gets up and leaves to go join his girlfriend.
END

GOOD ROOMMATE

NATALIE and ANNA are making a list of rules for the use of their apartment.

NATALIE

Okay, Anna. Rules for our apartment. No parties unless we both agree on a guest list.

ANNA

Agreed. And we keep the place neat and clean at all times.

NATALIE

Agreed. And we alternate weekend dustings, floor washings, and bathroom scrubbings.

ANNA

Agreed. We each do our own laundry, don't wear each other's clothes without permission, and only eat our own food from our own side of the refrigerator.

NATALIE

Absolutely. Oh, and we always pay the rent and utilities two weeks ahead of schedule, to be sure there aren't any errors.

ANNA

Good plan. Oh, don't forget television rules.

NATALIE

That's right. I get Mondays, Wednesdays, and Fridays, and we alternate Sundays.

ANNA

Very good. Well, I think we've got everything covered.

NATALIE

Except for one thing. When do you think we're ever going to actually get an apartment together?

ANNA

Maybe never, but it's still fun to plan. What do you want to do tonight?

NATALIE

I say we wear your sister's clothes and have a cheese puff fight in front of the TV.

ANNA
I'm not cleaning that mess.

NATALIE
Me, either. I call remote!

END

SWEET SHOES

Sisters SOPHIA and FAITH are discussing shoes in the living room.

SOPHIA
Those are some sweet shoes there, Faith.

FAITH
Thanks, Sophia. Do you think they go with my dress?

SOPHIA
Perfectly. Just the right shade of pink.

FAITH
Too tall?

SOPHIA
Just the right height.

FAITH
You don't think they're too gaudy?

SOPHIA
Not at all. In fact, I think they're very classy.

FAITH
I was thinking the same thing. We seem to have the same taste in shoes.

SOPHIA
We do, indeed. Want to know how I know that?

FAITH
How?

SOPHIA
Those are my shoes, from my closet, that I bought with my money. Now put them back and get your own shoes.

FAITH
Fine. I don't really like these, anyway. Got any purple shoes I can borrow?

SOPHIA
Put them back.

END

NUMBER, PLEASE?

DILLON and WILL are standing together in the mall.

DILLON
Will, don't tell me you didn't get her number.

WILL
Okay, I won't tell you.

DILLON
What happened? She shut you down? Did you chicken out? Listen, if you don't go over there and get her number, I'm gonna do it. I know she won't shut me down.

WILL
Don't do that, Dillon. I promise you, you won't be happy.

DILLON
Hey, if you haven't got the guts to ask her out, I will.

WILL
I did ask her out.

DILLON
What did she say?

WILL
She said she would, but only if I dumped my loser friend.

DILLON
Me?

WILL
You.

DILLON
I don't know what to say.

WILL
Wanna go get a burger, friend?

DILLON
Yeah, sounds good, friend.
END

BAD TUTOR

KIM and JADA are having a discussion before class.

KIM
Jada, did you know Nicki was a math tutor?

JADA
No. I didn't think she was that good at math.

KIM
Well, I'm not either, but I'm better at it than her.

JADA
How do you know that?

KIM
Because my mom wasn't happy with my grades, and told me I had to get a tutor.

JADA
So she had you go to Nicki?

KIM
Yeah. Can you believe that? And when I went to her house, she had me practice by doing her math homework. After the first couple lessons, I figured out what she was doing.

JADA
Did you tell her?

KIM
No. I decided to teach her a thing or two. I purposely wrote down all the wrong answers. She doesn't tutor math anymore, and her mom grounded her for getting bad grades.

JADA
Sounds like the tutor got tutored.

KIM
Yup. Oh, how the mighty have fallen.

END

FINAL NOTES

Go back and revisit these monologues and scenes from time to time. Look at them from different perspectives. Consider playing different characters in different environments and how your character could respond in different ways. Explore the possibilities.

Keep training, learning, practicing, and pursuing your craft. You are in charge of your career. No one else can do it for you. There are no shortcuts. Follow your dream, work hard, and most of all, have fun with it.

ABOUT THE AUTHOR

Dave Kilgore is an actor, pianist, film composer, music playwright, novelist, and lover of all the arts. He has written musical plays for kids, short and feature length screenplays and more.

Dave first appeared on the theatrical stage at the age of six, professionally on the sound stage as a pianist in a band at age fifteen, and as a film actor has been on camera in over one hundred film projects. These experiences, along with years of training, have given him the insight to write short monologues and scenes that are fresh, effective, and fun.

This book was inspired by a number of parents of young actors asking Dave where they could find good material for their kids to use for auditions and practice. After doing extensive research and finding so many pieces that were too long, poorly written, or age inappropriate, Dave decided to sit down and write his own monologues and scenes. His books have received high praise and have been sold in many countries.

Dave resides in Michigan, where he has been a staunch supporter of Michigan film for years, and remains deeply and proudly involved in the local industry.

You can contact Dave through his website, www.davekilgore.com.

CPSIA information can be obtained
at www.ICGtesting.com
Printed in the USA
LVHW020525040820
662268LV00017B/2535